The Real Truth About Mutual Funds

The Real Truth About Mutual Funds

And How to Make Money on Your Investments

Herbert Ringold

amacom

American Management Association

New York • Atlanta • Boston • Chicago • Kansas City • San Francisco • Washington, D. C.
Brussels • Mexico City • Tokyo • Toronto

This book is available at a special
discount when ordered in bulk quantities.
For information, contact Special Sales Department,
AMACOM, a division of American Management Association,
135 West 50th Street, New York, NY 10020.

This publication is designed to provide accurate and authoritative
information in regard to the subject matter covered. It is sold with the
understanding that the publisher is not engaged in rendering legal,
accounting, or other professional service. If legal advice or other expert
assistance is required, the services of a competent professional person
should be sought.

Library of Congress Cataloging-in-Publication Data

Ringold, Herbert.
    The real truth about mutual funds and how to make money on your
investments / Herbert Ringold.
        p.   cm.
    Includes bibliographical references and index.
    ISBN 0-8144-0314-X
    1. Mutual funds—United States.   I. Title.
HG4930.R56   1996
332.63'27—dc20   95-25342
                                                        CIP

Printing number

10   9   8   7   6   5   4   3   2   1

To **Evelyn,** my ex-wife: The feeling is "mutual."

And to **Margaret Russel,** my agent and honorary daughter.

Contents

An Unskippable Introduction

Would you, in your right mind, send your money to someone you didn't know and probably never heard of?

Would you agree that while he has your money, you have absolutely no control over what he does with it?

And would you accept the fact that he will be very well paid whether or not he makes a profit for you?

Further, do you understand that, should you change your mind, you will probably have to pay a fee just to get your money back?

Congratulations. You have just bought a mutual fund.

You have plenty of company.

One out of every four American households owns mutual funds.

Many of them made money.

Many of them lost money.

In the late '80s and early '90s, it was difficult not to make money with mutual funds. The rising tide of the bull market carried most of the boats with it—including the ponderous scows, the fragile canoes, even the leaking liners.

But then, a combination of an aging bull and Alan Greenspan of the Federal Reserve Board signaled the beginning of the end of the era of Easy Money. Most mutual funds lost money in 1994.

This book is being written in early 1995—too soon to be alarmed, too early to ask how now the Dow?

Will tougher times cause some mutual fund promoters to reduce their exorbitant fees, embrace truth in advertising, and stop treating the average investor as if he—only recently—fell off a turnip truck?

Doubtful.

Most mutual funds are honest and honorable. You can make a lot of money with carefully selected mutual funds, even when the stock market is turbulent and troublesome. Personally, I am dedicated to the viewpoint that mutual funds should be the investment of choice for most American families.

But there are a lot of bad guys out there. There are a great many dangers in mutual fund investing—some of which you may have never even heard about. Vigilance is not only the price of liberty, it is an absolute necessity if you plan on surviving.

Most books on mutual funds create the impression that all you have to do is send in your money and go out to price yachts. Most books on mutual funds are written by members of the Establishment. You seldom hear about the downside of mutual fund investing.

This book attempts to strike a balance between the financial benefits of mutual fund ownership and the frightening practices that can result in significant losses.

It will be irritating, boat-rocking, even exasperating.

But if you will give me half a chance, I can show you how to get rich—slowly.

The
Real Truth
About
Mutual Funds

One

Don't Buy Mutual Funds From a Stockbroker

Buying From a Broker Will Make You Broker

"Beware of false prophets which come to you in sheep's clothing, but inwardly they are raving wolves."

—Matthew 7:15

Repeat after me:

A broker is a salesman.
A broker is a salesman.
A broker is a salesman.

A broker works on commission. The higher the front-end load of a mutual fund he sells you, the more money the broker and his firm get to keep. None of the load goes to the mutual fund. Too often a broker will sell you what is in his best interest,

I

not yours. Ray Dirks, a stockbroker (reformed), wrote a book titled *The Case Against Your Broker*. He said:

> The average stockbroker is not the man you should listen to when you invest your money. Your interests and his interests are inherently contradictory.

No?

Consider the case of Broker Bob Rosenstock of Smith Barney, Los Angeles. The story of his "professional" mutual fund recommendations was published in *The New York Times* (November 19, 1994). Dina Defterious, age 25, earning just under $30,000 a year, asked him to recommend some mutual funds.

Rosenstock proposed that she put 40% of her money in the Investment Company of America Fund, 40% in the Capital Income Builder Fund, and 20% in the Euro-Pacific Growth Fund.

All of these funds have a front-end load of 5.75%.

More than 85% of all mutual funds have front-end loads of less than 5.75%. About 40% have no front-end loads at all. But Rosenstock, in all conscience, was unable to recommend any no-load funds. He makes no commission from no-load funds.

Sure, he is entitled to be paid something for his so-called expert advice. But not only were his recommended funds overloaded; neither were they particularly good.

Each Wednesday, *The Wall Street Journal* ranks the performance of all funds over a three-year period. On November 30, 1994, these rankings showed that none of the recommended funds had performed in the top 20% of their group.

Morningstar Mutual Fund Reports, the recognized authority in the field, said of the Capital Income Builder Fund: "Its overall first half results still trail the averages."

The Investment Company of America Fund did not earn Morningstar's 5-star rating. However, the Dodge & Cox Fund, in the same group, did earn this top ranking. Want to guess why the Dodge & Cox fund was not recommended?

Right. It's a no-load fund. Worse yet, there are many funds in the same general category with excellent performance records, sound management, and innovative investment styles that have lower front-end loads.

The Euro-Pacific Growth Fund is an emerging country fund whose risks and volatility are considerably higher than those for typical growth funds. How many of you would consider this a prudent recommendation for a young woman earning less than $30,000 a year?

Okay. This is an aberration. A deviation from the normal. One example proves nothing.

Maybe so, but, not according to Robert Metz, former "Market Place" columnist for *The New York Times,* who said in his book *Jackpot! Everything You Need to Know About Smart Money Investing in the New Wall Street:*

> Careful, dedicated brokers who handle accounts of less than $100,000 with tender, loving care are scarce enough that you need not waste your time looking for one. Someday, you may find one, but, in the meanwhile, those you rely on along the way may lose half of your capital.

Experts?

Most stockbrokers are not mutual fund experts. They can't be. They simply have too much else to do.

Their principal business is buying and selling stocks, which means that they must focus most of their efforts upon thousands of stocks on three different stock exchanges. They must be reasonably knowledgeable about options, warrants, indexes, puts and calls, and all of the new-fangled derivatives. They certainly need to be familiar with corporate, government, and municipal bonds. They need to follow—and understand—all the indices that indicate the direction of the economy and the stock market. Finally, they have to spend a lot of time talking to clients, soliciting new business, and buying and selling stocks and bonds.

How many of the more than 6,000 mutual funds can they really know much about?

What usually happens is that the brokerage firm nominates a few mutual funds and those are the ones the brokers sell— whether they suit your individual requirements or not.

Money magazine said:

> Too often brokerage firms come up with a product their brokers can easily sell rather than one suited to their customer's risk tolerance.

Forbes magazine, worried that some stockbrokers were "getting away with murder" in pushing mutual funds, had its reporters call 22 brokers throughout the country and indicate some interest in purchasing mutual funds from them. Much of the "advice" they received was either deceptive or simply a bunch of lies.

One broker in Texas said that nobody who had stayed in mutual funds for ten years or more had ever lost any money. Another broker, from a leading Wall Street firm, made the ridiculous claim that certificates of deposit are not insured. Yet another broker from another nationally known firm tried to sell his firm's own utilities fund by claiming that it was one of the better-performing funds available when, in fact, it had been at the bottom half of its category for the past five years.

Brokers work on commission, resulting, many times, in the omission of material information and the commission of acts of deception, subterfuge, and chicanery. In other words, some of them lie a lot.

Thieves?

At first, the following story does not seem to have much to do with why you should not buy mutual funds from a stockbroker. Would you trust me for a page or two?

Some big-name brokerage firms trade stocks and mutual

funds in-house. You place an order, and the brokerage firm fills it from its own inventory, at prices which are often higher than the current price quoted on the Exchange.

"It's like taking candy from a baby," said one trader. "All day our brokers get sell orders at, say, 6, and buy orders at $6^1/8$. We're minting money."

A lousy eighth of a point—is that minting money?

Is it ever!

This in-house trading is called 19c-3 trading, after the Securities and Exchange Commission regulation which permits it. Some of Wall Street's biggest firms have 19c-3 desks and they make a great deal of money. Like millions.

In order to point up the highly questionable morality of 19c-3 trading, it is necessary to explain how it works.

A given stock is trading with a spread of say, $5^1/4$ to $5^1/2$. You instruct your broker to buy the stock, and, in the best of all worlds, your sainted broker would (should) try to get you the best price.

Not at a lot of 19c-3 desks, however. There, your order is filled out of the firm's inventory without even making an effort to get you at least the mid-point between $5^1/4$ and $5^1/2$ a share. Your order is filled at $5^1/2$. Then the firm buys the stock on the exchange at the mid-point, keeping the extra eighth (or $12^1/2$ cents).

An eighth here and an eighth there. Remember the senator who said "A billion here, a billion there, soon you run into real money"? It has been reported in the financial press that these 19c-3 desks account for extra profits of more than $500 million a year. So what has all this to do with mutual funds?

The people who run these brokerage firms with their 19c-3 desks are the very same people who supervise and direct the brokers who sell you mutual funds. If they can accede to, or look away from, this thievery—and that's what it is—in one part of their office, how sure are you that the instructions they give their brokers who sell mutual funds are not similarly sleazy? The environment is polluted. The brokers know, or sense, that they are working for bosses who are "flexible" when it comes to making a dishonest dollar. What, then, are your chances of getting a square deal?

There is an old quotation on Wall Street that seems to apply here. A broker says of an investment he just sold to a client, "The firm made money. I made money. Two out of three isn't bad."

Loads vs. No-Loads

All right. You have this absolutely honest broker. He was a choir boy, an Eagle scout, you have known him for 25 years, and, compared to him, George Washington and Abraham Lincoln were both crooks.

Do not buy mutual funds from him. He is going to sell you a load fund.

Let's say that you invest $10,000 in a no-load fund and your brother invests $10,000 in a fund with an 8.5% front-end load. If each fund grows at 10% a year, at the end of just two years you will have earned $1,028 more than your brother. And every year thereafter, the spread between your profits and his will continue to widen.

Now hold on here. There are only a handful of funds with an 8.5% front-end load. The example cited is both arbitrary and unrealistic.

Fair enough.

A great many funds levy loads between 5.25% and 5.75%. But just to be absolutely fair, how about if we go down to a 5.0% load?

If you invest $20,000 in a 5% load fund, you give away $1,000 to start with. That means you are investing only $19,000 in the fund. Your fund has to earn more than 5.2% before you even break even!

Performance Comparisons

There are endless—endless—studies that show that load funds do not do any better than no-load funds. In fact, they do slightly worse.

A study by the University of Pennsylvania Wharton School of Finance for the Securities and Exchange Commission found "no evidence that higher sales charges go hand-in-hand with better investment performance." CDA/Weisenberger compared 82 no-load funds with 138 load funds. It found that:

> There was no significant different in risk, diversification, rate of return, or risk-adjusted performance over one-, three-, and five-year periods.

FundScope conducted an extensive study of loads vs. no-loads, covering income, growth, and stability. It concluded:

> In the end, because so many no-load and so many load funds perform above average and so many below average, you must reach the conclusion that there is just no relationship, no correlation between load and results.

Kiplinger's Personal Finance magazine reported:

> The statistics speak for themselves. Your odds of a superior total return are greatest with a no-load fund.

A. Michael Lipper of Lipper Analytical Services added:

> A look at the load-adjusted performance of front-end loads and no-load funds shows no-load funds with a definite edge in the performance derby.

Load funds do not necessarily get you superior performance. The principal thing they get you is a salesman.

In February 1995 *Forbes* magazine published its "Best Buys" in mutual funds. Of the 10 U.S. stock funds recommended, none was a load fund. Of the 10 balanced funds it recommended, 8 were no-loads. Of the 8 foreign stock funds it recommended, all were no-loads. Of the 8 global funds it recommended, 6 were no-loads. Out of its total of 36 recommended funds, 32 were no-load funds.

In the 1993 edition of *Business Week's Annual Guide to Mutual Funds,* funds were given one of seven ratings, depending on their five-year risk-adjusted performance. The two lowest ratings were Poor and Very Poor. A total of 130 funds received one of these two bottom ratings; 70% were load funds.

Morningstar writes an analysis of each mutual fund it covers. Here are 10 excerpts from these reports, each referring to a different fund:

Its long-term record is frighteningly bad.

The fund's trailing three-year numbers are unimpressive.

The fund's record over the past three years has been dismal.

This fund currently lands near the group's bottom.

Unfortunately, these measures haven't prevented the fund from going bust so far this year.

To date, this fund has been lackluster.

This fund has suffered a loss three times the group's average.

Only five other growth funds have recorded worse losses in 1994.

Last year's abysmal result shows how much the fund can underperform in adverse markets.

The fund posted the ninth-worst 1993 loss of all funds in Morningstar's data base.

Every one of these excerpts is taken from description of funds with a front-end load of 5% or more.

Every one of the above funds was sold by a stockbroker or a bank. The investors who bought them paid a hefty commission for: advice?

Mostly, the advice was: buy a load fund.

Discount Brokers

Having said all those terrible things about stockbroker who sell mutual funds, I now want to take some of it back.

Buying mutual funds from a discount stockbroker can be a good idea, provided that the funds available suit your needs.

Charles Schwab originated the no-transaction-fee mutual fund sale. He has since been joined by Jack White, Waterhouse, Muriel Siebert, and others, but Schwab is the biggest and the most efficient.

If you like any of the funds available to you through these discount brokers, you can buy them without paying a load. The discount broker gets paid $1/4$ of 1% by the fund for as long as you own your shares. The fund figures, quite reasonably, that paying this small percentage is less expensive than its advertising and marketing costs would be if it promoted the funds itself. And it gets an automatic sales organization with offices throughout the country.

At Schwab, you can buy about 300 different funds without paying a load, including some of the most illustrious names in the mutual fund industry. If the fund you want is not on Schwab's list, you can still buy it from him for a minimum charge of $29 or 0.6% of the principal up to $15,000 worth of shares.

There are thousands of mutual funds you can buy without paying a load by dealing directly with the given fund—what's the big deal about going to a discount broker?

Convenience.

Let's say you want to buy a growth fund, a balanced fund, and an international fund—but they come from three different fund families.

You are up to here in paperwork. You get three different statements at the end of the month. If you have questions, you have to make three different phone calls and talk to three different tape recordings called Voice Mail. (Why is it that people with Voice Mail are always out?)

With a discounter, you get one statement covering all your transactions.

There are other problems that result from buying a little bit here and a little bit there. Let's say you own a Fidelity fund which you now want to sell and replace with a Vanguard fund. You call Fidelity, tell them to sell your shares, and wait for a check to arrive. Then you wait for it to clear. Then you have to call Vanguard and write them a check. A week or more may pass before all these transactions are completed, and you are out of action during that time, perhaps missing some upward moves. At Schwab, one phone call is all you need to switch among the funds he offers.

It is necessary to add quickly that a recent development at Fidelity has considerably reduced this Schwab advantage. Now you can choose from more than 350 non-Fidelity funds, buy them from Fidelity, and enjoy all of the privileges that were once a Schwab exclusive. Fidelity's "Funds Network" offers such non-Fidelity funds as Berger, Gabelli, Janus, Kaufmann, Montgomery, Stein-Roe, Strong, and Warburg Pincus. And you can intermingle any of these with Fidelity funds. One call does it all (1-800-544-9697).

Banks

In considering the question whether to buy mutual funds from banks, I started by talking to Don Phillips, publisher of *Morningstar Mutual Fund Reports* and universally recognized as one of the most authoritative voices in the industry. He said:

> Over the past decade, banks have made their money by lending. The new generation, however, is more interested in saving and investing. The banks didn't want to be left out. However, I don't think the banks have really thought through what business they are getting into. They are trying to cash in on their reputation without really understanding the mutual fund industry.

About a year ago, a big Midwestern bank came to Morningstar and made a big presentation to us about their entrance into the mutual fund industry. But all they talked about was how profitable it was going to be and how much money they were going to make. They made no reference at all to the quality of the products they were going to sell, no reference to their marketing strategy, no reference to how they were going to help the average investor. All they discussed were their profits—not the potential profits of their customers. I don't think they cared.

Then, I started my own investigation of banks that sell mutual funds.

I visited the main branch of the PNC bank in downtown Philadelphia, one of the city's largest banking organizations. I was directed to Nancy Hornberger.

I told her that I was retired and was interested in some conservative mutual funds that offer some growth potential along with a stream of dividends.

After a few questions—a very few questions—she recommended the Putnam Growth and Income Fund.

Does it surprise you that the Putnam Growth and Income Fund has one of the industry's highest loads—5.75%? (There are fewer than 10 funds with a higher front-end load.)

As she enumerated the merits of this fund—the usual clichés—I kept reminding her that I was interested only in a conservative fund. Her head kept bobbing up and down every time I used the word "conservative," and she finished her pitch with the statement that she had sold this fund to a lot of people who were conservative investors.

What she didn't tell me was that:

1. The fund invested in junk bonds. On page 7 of the prospectus is the statement:

   The Fund may invest in lower rated fixed-income securities, regardless of credit rating.

Gulp.

2. The fund invested in put and call options.
3. The fund invested in stock index futures.
4. The fund speculated in foreign currencies. Page 7 of the prospectus states:

> The fund may buy or sell foreign currencies and foreign currency forward contracts for hedging purposes in connection with its foreign investments.

There is nothing inherently wrong with any of the procedures described above. Many well-established funds have made profits (and losses) by using them. But would you call them conservative? Would you call them ideal for a retired investor who reemphasized his interest only in a conservative fund?

You might, if you were earning a 5.75% commission.

For years, I had my checking account at the Mellon bank in suburban Philadelphia. I called my branch office and said I would like some information about mutual funds. A meeting was arranged with James Ryan, the mutual fund "expert."

All I told Ryan was that I was interested in mutual funds because I needed something more than certificates of deposit and money market accounts to keep up with the rising cost of living.

He did not ask me any questions. He did not inquire about my general financial condition, marital status, children, outstanding debts, or my attitude about risk.

He immediately recommended the Dreyfus Disciplined Stock Fund. And he made a very big point of the fact that it was a no-load fund.

A no-load fund from a bank? A no-load fund from a salesman?

Answer: Mellon owns Dreyfus.

He gave me a handout from the fund, showing its recent performance. I glanced through it and said: "I notice that the funds offers two kinds of shares—Investor shares and R. shares. What are they, and what is the difference between them?"

He did not know. After searching through various brochures and turning endless pages, he finally said that one class of shares had more expenses than the others.

Wrong. Incorrect. Not true. And that is the bank's mutual fund "expert."

Oh, by the way, the Dreyfus Disciplined Stock Fund lost money in 1994.

I was amused by a sentence in one of the promotional pieces I was given. Please note: the following sentence is reproduced exactly as it appears. What you are about to read is not a typographical error:

> Historically, socks or equtiy funds have proved to be the most effective investment against inflation.

English teachers of the world, arise. Do not buy mutual funds from a bank that cannot spell. "Equtiy" funds may be a good investment, but I am not so sure about "socks."

In both of these situations, the "experts" took the easy way out. They each recommended only one fund. Diversification is one of the keys to success in mutual fund investing. That, however, would have required considerable extra effort.

I told the young woman at the PNC bank that I had $25,000 to invest. If I had bought the fund she recommended with its 5.75% load, her bank would have collected $1,425 up front. For that kind of money, one might think that some extra effort is warranted.

Lest you think that these two personal experiences are just unfortunate coincidences, you should read the article titled "Should You Buy Mutual Funds From Your Bank?" in the March 1994 issue of *Consumer Reports*. It investigated 40 banks in five states and found a lot of poor advice and—there is no other way to put it—a lot of lying.

A salesman from one of New York City's leading banks stated that a 10% return was guaranteed! A representative from a Los Angeles bank said that his bank's mutual funds were completely safe, and would provide a 20% return with little, if any, risk. Many of the salesmen claimed that insurance from the Securities Investor Protection Corporation, provided by many banks, was just as good as FDIC insurance. The fact is that the SIPC does not insure the performance of investments. It insures brokerage firms, but pays off only if the brokerage firm goes bankrupt.

Only six of the 40 salespeople asked the appropriate investigative questions and made prudent recommendations, leading *Consumer Reports* to conclude that "the odds of getting good advice at a bank that sells mutual funds are worse than 1 in 6."

Then there is the case of Leilani DeMint, a single mother from St. Petersburg, Florida. Her certificate of deposit, worth $57,000, was about to mature, so she called some banks to see which one would offer the best rates when she reinvested the money in another CD.

One of the banks she called had sold her the certificate of deposit. She was told that that bank could beat all the rates the other banks were quoting, and she was advised to let the bank purchase government bonds for her.

DeMint transferred her CD and wrote an additional check for $3,000, thinking she was buying U.S. savings bonds. Six months later, she got a statement from a company she had never heard of.

She called to inquire and was told, according to *Modern Maturity* magazine, that:

> She had bought mutual funds and was lucky she hadn't lost more than $1,000 of the principal.

Things have come to a pretty pass when even your Uncle Sam is worried about all this. In 1995, the Federal Deposit Insurance Corporation announced that it was organizing a group of undercover agents to visit banks selling mutual funds in an effort to eliminate these flagrant abuses. And legislation has been introduced in Congress to rein in the "enthusiasm" of banks.

Most banks have a limited list of funds they make available for sale. And the selection of which funds get onto the so-called preferred list is not necessarily based on what is best for the customer. It is based on what funds benefit the bank.

Benefit the bank? In what way?

Money.

Some funds are made available by some banks only after the fund has agreed to pay the bank 2.5 cents of every dollar of the fund sold by the bank.

The fund may—or may not—be suitable for you. The fund may—or may not—be as good as other funds who refuse to pay this ransom.

Illegal? Probably not—the funds piously claim that they are merely contributing to the banks' distribution costs.

Immoral? Unethical?

So what else is new?

Some banks have even started their own mutual funds. Banks that lost their shirts (your shirt?) by making bad real estate loans have now suddenly become stock market gurus. They charge outrageous percentages on their credit cards, close branch offices and reduce service personnel, and levy all kinds of fees on savings and checking accounts. And now they are more trustworthy than Fidelity or Vanguard?

Forbes magazine, not exactly a wild-eyed radical publication, wrote:

"Are bank funds good buys? In a word, no."

A Survey

In November 1993 the Securities and Exchange Commission released the results of a survey it conducted to determine if investors were clear about mutual funds purchased through stockbrokers or banks.

Thirty-six percent of the respondents believed that mutual funds purchased from a stockbroker are federally insured.

Twenty-eight percent of the respondents believe that all mutual funds sold through banks are federally insured, like savings accounts and CDs.

Thirty percent of the respondents thought that mutual funds sold through banks are safer than other mutual funds.

Mutual funds sold by brokers are not federally insured.

Mutual funds sold by banks are not federally insured.

Mutual funds sold by banks are not safer than other mutual funds.

No mutual funds are federally insured.

Some mutual funds buy United States Treasury bills, notes, or bonds. United States Treasury bills, notes, or bonds are insured by the full faith and credit of the United States Government. That means that the government positively will pay the full amount of the financial instrument to the fund upon maturity and will positively pay whatever interest rate is indicated.

Period.

Questions to Ask

If, despite my screaming and yelling and jumping up and down, you still are considering buying mutual funds from a stockbroker or a bank, please make note of the following questions that you should be asked:

1. Why do you want to invest in mutual funds?
2. What is your age and marital status? Do you have children? What are their ages?
3. What is your approximate household income? Mortgage? Do you have other significant debts? Other investments?
4. How do you feel about risk?
5. Do you need monthly income?

If you are not asked most of those questions, do not stop to grab your hat. Just git.

Here is a list of questions that you should ask:

1. Before you even sit down, ask, "Which mutual funds do you recommend?" If the salesperson answers that question, don't even sit down. Out. No one—no one—can recommend any mutual funds without knowing a great deal about you.
2. When, eventually, a recommendation is made, ask, "What is the load?" If the load is more than 5%, you are being taken. If you are told there is no load, smile and say, "Please tell me about the 12b-1 charges and any other fees that apply for as long as I own my shares."
3. "How many stars has this fund received from Morningstar?" This is not an absolute, but why are you buying two- and three-star funds when there are plenty of four- and five-star funds?

Don't buy anything then and there. The salesperson is legally required to give you a prospectus and ask you if you have read it, before he can take your money. And please see Chapter 9 on understanding the prospectus.

Your Legal Rights

I would like to offer you some advice about your legal rights, should you have any complaints against stockbrokers, banks that sell mutual funds, or the mutual funds themselves.

When you open an account with a stockbroker, you will be asked to sign an agreement. You will probably be told that it is "just routine."

Don't sign it!

There will be a paragraph in it which says something to this effect:

It is agreed that any controversy between us arising out of our business or this Agreement will be submitted to arbitration.

Offhand, that sounds perfectly reasonable. If there is a significant disagreement, it will be settled by some neutral arbiters. Sort of like going to court, where both sides are heard and a judicial decision is reached.

No. No. No. No. No. No. No. No.

If you sign any agreement containing the essence of that paragraph, you are giving up your right to go to court. You are required to go to arbitration and you cannot Sue The Bastards.

You have two chances of winning at arbitration: slim and none. Despite what anyone tells you—particularly a stockbroker—the arbiters are usually not neutral. They usually have exactly the same background as the defendants, and there is often a very cozy relationship between them. Many arbiters are lawyers and accountants who work for brokers; most are associated with the securities industry. There is no appeal. You have had it.

There is a very easy way to protect yourself. Just make a small change in the paragraph cited above. After the word "controversy," insert the phrase "except state and federal law claims."

By adding that phrase, you will not have given up your right to go to court. Without the phrase, you absolutely cannot seek relief in a court of law.

Initial the change, and have your brokers add his initials also. And be sure you don't leave until you have a copy of the agreement in your hands.

The Securities and Exchange Commission

If you have a complaint against a mutual fund, there is a course of action open to you which, unfortunately, many people don't know about. You can call the Office of Consumer Affairs of the Securities and Exchange Commission (1-800-942-0022).

This office, unlike many governmental bureaucracies, will really help you. It is sympathetic, cooperative, and very user-friendly.

If your complaint has any reasonable basis, the SEC will get in touch with the indicated mutual fund and attempt to arrange a resolution of your problem. Should a mutual fund official be unresponsive, this office can turn your complaint over to one of its field office inspectors for further action. There are not many mutual funds that look forward to official visits from a Securities and Exchange Commission inspector.

In 1994 complaints made to this office against mutual funds increased 46% over the preceding year. I would not say that this is an outstanding vote of confidence in this supposedly squeaky clean industry.

The Office of Consumer Affairs categorized all the complaints it received in 1994 against mutual funds. Which is the leading one?

Delays in the transfer of securities. Suppose, for example, that you own shares in Fund A in a family of funds. You call to say you would like to sell those shares and put the resultant money in Fund B in the same family. The fund evidently doesn't make the transfer in a timely fashion. You moved your shares into Fund B because you thought the price would go up. It goes up—but the fund has not yet made the transfer and you do not enjoy the benefits of the recent gain.

The second largest group of complaints was "misrepresentation of guarantees of performance."

Aha! All those pie-in-the-sky brokers. All those mutual fund salespeople in banks. And all that deceptive mutual fund advertising you can read about in Chapter 4.

Just as I was about to conclude this chapter, I heard Bing Crosby singing, "Life's highway is not covered with flowers."

Sad and true.

One of the purposes of this book is to help you prevent people trampling all over your flowers.

Two

Don't Buy Mutual Funds on the Basis of Past Performance Alone

Past Performance Is for Horses

"You can't look in the rear-view mirror to see where you are going."

—Mario Andretti, Indy 500 winner

It is 1987.

You are reading the annual *Forbes* magazine Honor Roll of Mutual Funds. You decide to invest in each of the 19 funds that has won the industry's most-distinguished award.

Then you go to sleep for seven years.

You wake up in 1994, on the very day that the *Forbes* Honor Roll is published (September 1994—the last honor roll available before this book went to press).

Ninety-five percent of the original list has disappeared. The once leading funds are now the new lagging funds.

But, you say, selecting 1987 as the beginning year is an arbitrary decision that proves only that you can prove anything if you set your own ground rules. And seven years is too long a time period.

All right. How about five years?

In 1990 19 funds were selected for the *Forbes* Honor Roll. Only four of them were still on the Honor Roll in 1994—about 80% had fallen by the wayside.

Well, as the time frame gets shorter, certainly those winning funds will continue to be winners.

It ain't necessarily so.

Twenty funds were on the Honor Roll in 1991. Only three of them were selected again in 1994. That means that about 85% of them had disappeared—in just four years.

The percentage is only slightly better over a three-year time span. Of the 19 funds on the 1992 Honor Roll, five made it again in 1994—a vanishing act covering about 75% of the original funds.

In the articles that accompany the Honor Roll, *Forbes* itself repeatedly—repeatedly—warns its readers of the dangers of assuming that good past performance ensures future profitability.

In 1987 *Forbes* wrote:

And so it is with mutual funds. Some perform spectacularly one year and sink the next.

In 1990 it wrote:

Past performance," the prospectus always says, "is not representative of future results." Boy, is that ever true! Past performance is only a weak indicator of future results.

In 1991 it wrote:

You can usually bet that this year's hot performer will be next year's laggard.

Would you like some further proof?

In 1989 the Lexington Strategic Investment fund produced a 61.23% return. In 1990 it lost 43.35%.

In 1989 the Sherman Dean fund gained 47.27%. In 1990 it was minus 44.14%.

In 1989 Twentieth Century Vista had a 52.20% profit. In 1990 it had a 15.73% loss.

In 1991 Invesco Strategic Health Sciences delivered an astounding 91.80% gain. In 1990, it lost 14.40%.

In 1991 Fidelity Select Biotechnology produced an eye-popping 99.05% increase. The next year it lost 10.34%.

Actually, Fidelity Select Biotechnology was not the biggest winner in 1991. Oppenheimer Global Biotechnology did even better, with an unbelievable increase of 121%. But in 1992 Wall Street found some new toys, and this Oppenheimer fund lost 23%.

In 1993 Fidelity's Emerging Markets Fund was plus 82%. In 1994 it lost 17.9%.

In 1993 American Heritage had a 41.3% profit. In 1994 it was one of the biggest losers of all funds, with a 34.9% deficit.

The Dreyfus Strategic Growth Fund is a perfect example of funds that go up and down like a yo-yo. In 1987, despite the market crash on Black Monday, it gained 63%. Investors, looking for a ship that was not sinking, got on board in record numbers. In the next two years, however, the fund trailed the S&P 500 by a double-digit percentage. In the following two years, it lost 7.15% and 15.36%, respectively. (Or disrespectively.) And in early 1993, things were so bad that the fund's assets had fallen to just a fourth of their 1988 peak.

Then—ah, but you already guessed—the fund turned around again and was one of the few to post a 1994 profit.

Okay, so some funds are rather volatile, but, generally speaking, the good funds rise to the top and stay there.

Sometimes.

How many funds made the *Forbes* Honor Roll for eight consecutive years?

None.

How many funds made the *Forbes* Honor Roll for seven consecutive years?

One (the Guardian Park Avenue Fund).

Besides Guardian, how many funds made the Honor Roll for six consecutive years?

One (Fidelity Destiny 1).

Objection!

Practically nobody would buy all the 18 or 20 funds which make up the *Forbes* Honor Roll each year. How about if we just focus on each year's winners and trace their forward progress?

In 1987 Fidelity's Magellan Fund produced the highest returns of all the funds on the Honor Roll that year. For the succeeding two years, it continued to lead all the other funds in annual profit percentage. Then it totally disappeared from the Honor Roll.

In 1990 Phoenix Growth led the Honor Roll with the highest percentage gain—22.1%. In 1992 and 1993, its yearly return was under 5%, and in 1994 it lost money.

In 1991 the T. Rowe Price International Fund was the winner, with a 20.4% gain. In 1992 it was a loser, dropping 3.47%.

In 1992 the winner was Bergstrum Capital, a closed-end fund which trades on the American Stock Exchange. It ended 1994 12% off its high.

The 1993 and 1994 winner was Merrill Lynch Pacific A.

In the period from 1987 through 1994, 35 funds made the Honor Roll—and were never heard of again. Of the 20 funds on the 1994 Honor Roll, 14 had never been on it before, ever.

Questions About the Honor Roll

Problem.

Time out to explain problem.

Forbes magazine uses some very complicated and arbitrary computations to determine the funds that are eligible for its Honor Roll.

If a fund, in a given year, produces the highest annual return of all other funds, it does not necessarily make the Honor Roll. *Forbes* takes into account such things as continuity of management, performance in both bull and bear markets, management expenses, and exposure to risk, among other factors. It eliminates all sector funds. In the year that the Franklin Utilities Fund and the Century Shares Fund achieved "market-beating" results, neither was included.

There is nothing wrong with the *Forbes* method of picking its winners. It tells you the rules in advance, explains them carefully, and supports its conclusions with convincing evidence—as *Forbes* sees it.

However, there are those of us who don't need all those complications and complexities. Just tell us which fund produced the highest return each year and—using only that information—let us see if we can profit from past performance.

Let's go back, as we did with the Honor Roll, to 1987, pick the most profitable fund each year, and demonstrate how it did as the years rolled by. No statistical weightings, no arbitrary eliminations, no consideration of risk—just which fund produced the most profits.

In 1987 the fund that returned the most profits was the USAA Investment Gold Fund, with an incredible return of 127.5%. It was closely followed by the Van Eck Gold Fund, which had a 126.2% return. Those are not exactly shabby performances, particularly when the S&P 500 had only a 25.1% gain.

Neither of these funds ever won the most profitable title again. The very next year, USAA Investment Gold lost 17.11%. The Van Eck Gold Fund was minus 21.33%.

In 1988 the most profitable fund was G.T. Global New Pacific Growth, with a gain of 48.12%. That was exceptional—the S&P 500 lost 6.9% that year.

The very next year, G.T. Global New Pacific Growth showed a loss of 10.96%. From 1989 through 1994 it had a deficit every other year.

In 1989 the winner and new champion was the Eagle Growth Fund, with a 51.8% return. It then slowly but steadily started to go in reverse and ended 1994 with a 15.4% loss. It was ranked by *The Wall Street Journal* in the bottom 20% of its category.

In 1990 the fund that, like Abou Ben Adem, led all the rest was the Scudder New Asia Fund, with a 58.6% return. The following year, it barely managed to turn a profit, ending the year plus a magnificent 0.3%. (Subsequently, this fund merged and changed its name, so there are no continuing individual results).

In 1991 Fidelity Biotechnology was first with a gain of 99.05%. In 1992 it lost money.

In 1992 it was the turn of the Fidelity Select Bank Fund to top the profitability list, with a 48.5% increase. The fund's profit was considerably reduced in 1993; in 1994 the fund showed a loss.

For 1993 the top honors went to the Evergreen Global Real Estate Equity Fund, with a 51.42% advance. The following year it lost 12.9%.

The 1994 winner was Seligman Communications. (How is it doing now?)

So what have we here?

From 1987 through 1994, no fund repeated as the winner in the competition to show the highest one-year results.

One year, it's a gold fund, then an international fund, then a growth fund, then a Pacific fund, then a biotechnology fund, then a bank fund, and, finally, a communications fund.

Longer-Term Performance

There must be some way to use past performance as an infallible yardstick to predict future profitability. How about funds with an outstanding five-year record? Wouldn't five years of continuous gains prove beyond a shadow of a doubt that the fund had a solid game plan and was an odds-on bet to deliver profits in the sixth year?

Not necessarily.

Here are just a few examples, of which, unfortunately, there are many more:

The Oppenheimer Global Fund had a five-year cumulative record of plus 38.44%. In 1994 it lost 27.45%.

The Fidelity Select Biotechnology Fund produced an outstanding five-year record of plus 112.94%. In 1994 it lost 18.18%.

The CGM Capital Development Fund had an even better five-year record—plus 135.42%. It also had a bigger 1994 loss—minus 22.92%.

How about 10 years?

The Wall Street Journal (January 6, 1995) printed a list of the 50 funds with the best 10-year records. Certainly funds that had weathered all the storms over 10 years, including Black Monday in 1987, would be sure to continue producing profits.

(I apologize.) Not necessarily.

The Acorn Fund had a ten-year gain of 362.41%. In 1994 it lost 7.45%.

Fidelity Select Leisure had a 10-year profit of plus 395.57%. In 1994 it lost 6.79%.

CGM Capital Development's 10-year cumulative record was a handsome plus 502.28%. In 1994 it lost 22.92%.

The Cam International Fund had the third-best record of all funds over a 10-year period, plus 574.32%. In 1994 it lost 10.23%.

Then there is the sad story of the 44 Wall Street Fund. Over ten years, it racked up a total return of plus 364%. In the next 10 years, it lost a total of 731%, making it the decade's worst-performing mutual fund.

Said the *Los Angeles Times:*

Past returns are not a good indication of future performance. A stunning, short-term performance often indicates that the fund is taking big risks and you are just as likely to lose big as you are to gain.

And *The Wall Street Journal* observed that hot funds cool off with disturbing regularity.

Finally, Donald Christensen, in his book *Surviving the Coming Mutual Fund Crisis,* wrote:

> Don't put your money in a fund that appears on the top of any chart measuring recent performance. The list of top performers on last quarter's performance charts is best used to identify the funds you don't want to be in. You can be fairly certain without further investigation that the ones at the top are either juiced up to the hilt with the riskiest types of tricks available or are representing some small volatile part of the market.

A Wolf in Sheep's Clothes?

There is another very significant factor which tends to muddle past performance figures and make some of them meaningless.

You have seen advertising claims by many funds which state:

"#1 in the Category"

"Ranked 2nd in the Fund Group by Lipper"

"#1 Out of 52 Funds in the Same Category"

John Bogle, chairman of Vanguard, had just a few words to say about these rankings. His comment:

> The greatest bunch of baloney foisted on the American public in years.

Them's fightin' words—what is Bogle so riled up about?

The Warburg Pincus Growth and Income Fund was ranked as the fourth-best performer out of 387 growth and income funds in 1994. And it was ranked second over the three-year period from 1990 to 1993.

That is a damn good record. Investors searching for a likely growth and income fund would have to give some serious consideration to that performance record.

Except the Warburg Pincus Growth and Income Fund is not a growth and income fund.

Said Adam Wright, a Morningstar analyst, "It is an aggressive growth fund in disguise."

The Warburg Pincus fund achieved its excellent record by investing in stocks totally atypical for its group. The lead investments of the growth and income group in 1994 were such stocks as General Electric, Philip Morris, and Xerox. Warburg Pincus made its money by taking a chance on such high fliers as Micron Technology, Storage Technology, and National Semi-Conductor.

There is absolutely nothing wrong with those stocks. But if you were searching for a solid, substantial growth and income fund, you might not want one that bought risky technology stocks, a category normally shunned by the group. If you wanted an aggressive growth fund, you could have bought one. In this, and in many other similar cases, you would be buying the investment style of an aggressive growth fund whether you wanted it or not.

Some fund watchers feel that there are elements of a real scandal here. Do some funds intentionally miscategorize themselves in order to produce a misleading past performance record that puts them at the top of the class—a class they don't belong to in the first place?

As *Worth* magazine said:

The best way to win a contest for the largest tomato is to paint a cantaloupe red.

There is considerable evidence that miscategorizing is rampant throughout the mutual fund industry.

Eric Witkowski, of Northfield Information Services, examined the performance of 709 equity funds over a five-year period. He found that 56% were misclassified. Of the 20 top-ranked growth funds, 14 were really aggressive growth funds. Of the top 20 growth and income funds, nine should have been typed either as small-company funds or aggressive growth funds, both considerably riskier than the more stolid growth and income category.

Dan DiBartolemeo, president of Northfield, said:

> High-risk wolves disguise themselves as low-risk sheep to outperform their "peers" when markets are booming, while low-risk sheep slip into high-risk categories to look stellar when markets tumble.

"Objectives"

Fund managers are able to pick the spots they want because each fund is usually categorized by the fund itself when it defines its "objective" in its prospectus. However, most of these objectives have become utterly meaningless as fund managers range far and wide to make investments that are precisely contrary to the fund's objective, its category, or even its name.

The Alliance North American Government Income Fund is a terrifying example of this strange misclassification.

The Alliance North American Government Income Fund— what does that name suggest to you? A very conservative fund investing in United States Treasuries and similar governmental issues?

As of December 1994, this fund had 24% of its assets in Argentina! (Its shares ranked 101st out of 101 funds in Morningstar's worldwide bond category.)

The Montgomery Global Communications fund invests in "equities of communications companies."

At the end of 1994, 36% of its money was in utilities, 19% in service companies, and 11% in consumer durables.

What would you guess all the following funds have in common?

Delaware Dorchester
Fidelity Capital and Income

Kemper Diversified Income
National Bond
Nicholas Income
Northeast Investors

Business Week magazine says they are "junk bonds by other names."

The prospectus of the Mather Fund states that it invests "principally in common stocks."

The last time more than 50% of its holdings was in common stocks was in 1989.

The Evergreen Fund says that it seeks "companies that are little known, relatively small or special situations."

Its lead investments are Merck and Johnson & Johnson.

Perhaps the final word on this subject comes from Morningstar's John Rekenthaler. He discovered a biotechnology fund that owned shares in Ben & Jerry's Ice Cream. The fund manager admitted that neither Ben nor Jerry had anything to do with biotechnology—he just liked the stock.

Probably liked ice cream, too.

The Past . . . and the Future

One of the biggest problems with buying funds with the best five- or ten-year records is that you thereby eliminate the slow, steady, solid-performing funds that just keep on growing. No spectacular fireworks, but no ulcers, either. And if you inspect many of those great ten-year records, you often find that they have resulted from unusually profitable returns in the first five years, whereupon the fund starts to show its age.

The Changing Economic Situation

A much more important point, however, is that the economic climate is changing. There are new forces at play, many of them still unclear. The factors that drove some funds to the top 5 and 10, years ago, have been largely replaced by developments that were unknown in those days. Wall Street has a bad memory. It is constantly looking for new playthings.

Seligman Communications A was the most profitable fund in 1994, mostly because it owned the best-performing technology stocks. Will the Information Superhighway come up with some amazing innovations that will make these very stocks lose their luster? It has happened before—and before that, and before that.

What is the future for health funds? The economics of medicine is changing everyday. Will the emerging country funds finally live up to their promise? If Fed Chairman Alan Greenspan is not successful in stemming inflation, will the gold funds have their day once again? Or are you safer in balanced funds, index funds, asset allocation funds?

You cannot answer those questions by looking backward.

Sure, you should give some consideration to past performance. Just don't overdo it. There are too many other significant factors to take into account.

You are about to enter the twenty-first century. There are hundreds of new funds that don't have a 10-year—or even a five-year—record, and many of them hold out the promise of fantastic gains as they cross the new frontiers.

If you focus on the past, you may miss the future.

Had you been interested in mutual funds in the late '70s or early '80s, the fund promoters could not have impressed you with dazzling performance records. The records were frightful. Investors who bought mutual funds in those days did so despite the funds' previous histories. If, back in those dear, dead days beyond recall, an investor was smart and picked the right funds that suited his individual requirements, he made a handsome profit, regardless of the fact that his selections had a mediocre, even a poor past record. If, then, you had paid no attention to past performance records and bought funds that were investing in emerging industries, you would be reading this book on your yacht.

Throughout the late '80s and early '90s, the United States enjoyed the ideal economic circumstances for a roaring bull market—low interest rates and little or no inflation. People who owned certificates of deposit turned to mutual funds for better returns, and the incredible sums of money they poured in helped the stock market go on a rampage. In 1991 the average aggressive growth fund—the average fund—earned 54.49%.

The astounding numbers produced by mutual funds during a period of low interest rates and low inflation have nothing whatsoever to do with what they may produce when those conditions no longer exist.

Play it again, Sam: the astounding numbers produced by mutual funds during a period of low interest rates and low inflation have nothing whatsoever to do with what they may produce when those conditions no longer exist.

Do not overfocus on past performance.

Three

Don't Buy a 12b-1 Fund—and Watch Out for All Those Extra Charges

"To pay their fees, we need a bank."
                                    —"Calomel," Stanza I

Mutual funds get you coming and going—and even while you're standing still.

You are subjected to endless charges, which can add up to serious money.

The most vicious of these charges is known as 12b-1, which stands for the paragraph in the regulations of the Securities and Exchange Commission that gives mutual funds permission to take your money for no reason whatsoever.

Prior to the enactment of 12b-1, if a mutual fund wanted to advertise and promote its products, pay commissions to salespeople, and defray other unspecified expenses, the money for such expenditures was put up by the fund itself, out of its profits.

Not any more.

Now you pay these charges. The total amount of these costs

comes right off the top. It is deducted from the net asset value of the fund, and you get less money when you decide to sell your shares.

You were just mugged in broad daylight.

It may not come as a shock to you that the little fellow gets the shaft—again. But the history of this insidious 12b-1 charge may surprise you because there are two different versions—the official one and the real story.

It seems probable that the then commissioner of the SEC did not wake up one morning, have a fight with his wife, and decide that he was going to get even with all those stupid mutual fund investors by passing a regulation that makes them pay for charges previously borne by the mutual fund operators.

Getting the official version of the events which led up to the crime is not very difficult. All you have to do is read through 525 pages of a book issued by the SEC, titled, incredibly, *Protecting Investors*.

Starting on page 320 (the first 319 pages are not exactly like reading Danielle Steele) is the following:

> By the mid 1970s, the no-load segment of the industry had increased significantly. The distribution expenses of these no-load funds were borne by the investment advisors. As the popularity and number of no-loads increased, several of these funds requested that the staff take a no-action position, allowing them to use fund assets to pay for distribution. These requests were generally denied in accordance with the traditional position of the Commission that the use of fund assets to pay the costs of distributing fund shares was improper.

You mean to tell me that here is a governmental agency standing firm on behalf of the average investor in face of an onslaught from big-business interests?

Please do not rise for a standing ovation. The plot sickens.

The SEC report continues:

The industry nevertheless continued to press its view, pointing to the increase in net redemptions in some segments of the fund industry, the growing resistance to high front-end sales loads and the rising popularity of no-load funds. It argued that the rigidity of the regulatory approach for fund distribution put mutual funds at a disadvantage to competing investment products that could be offered to investors without such sales loads. The industry also argued that the use of fund assets for distribution expenditures would result in a net cash inflow into funds and in turn, economies of scale and more effective portfolio management.

The Commission adopted rule 12b-1 in 1980.

Shall we take a little closer look at the industry's arguments?

> . . . pointing to an increase in net redemptions in some segments of the fund industry
>
> growing resistance to high front-end sales loads
>
> rising popularity of no-load funds

Just picture it. Here come these greedy fund promoters who have been getting away with outrageous high front-end sales loads. Now they are whining that the public is actually resisting being overcharged. The no-load funds that aren't gouging investors have an unfair advantage over we poor, hapless, put-on millionaires. Some people are trampling on the American flag by redeeming their shares in protest. Where is Marie Antoinette now that we need her?

Further, they say, because these no-load funds are attracting lots of buyers, our business is off and that is—horrors—cutting into our profits. You couldn't possibly want that to happen to us. The only way we can get our money back is to make those suckers pay and pay and pay. Let 'em eat cake—let them pay our expenses. Otherwise, you will kill the hallowed spirit of the free enterprise system. Our forefathers who founded this nation would have amended the Constitution to include the right to steal, if they had known about mutual funds.

Their arguments continue:

> Use of fund assets for distribution expenses would re-sult in a net flow of cash into funds.

Alice in Wonderland. If the SEC will allow the funds to charge investors for expenses that the funds used to pay, then these investors will send in more money.

Does that make any sense to you?

Do you feel insulted and demeaned? Has your faith in the trustworthiness of mutual funds been reduced? Do I hear you saying "pirates," "robber barons," even "crooks"?

economies of scale

Economies of scale, my foot. Money has been pouring into mutual funds for year and their expenses, on average, have gone up, not down.

Said Don Phillips, publisher of the *Morningstar Mutual Fund Reports:*

> The benefits of the tremendous economies of scale un-leashed during the past decade were not shared with the fund shareholders.

The SEC report continues:

more effective portfolio management

If that weren't so sad, it would be funny: if you allow us to charge the investors with the expenses we used to pay, then we will have enough money left over to hire better portfolio man-agers.

I was under the impression that the funds already had

pretty good portfolio managers. Otherwise, why was I sending them my money?

Well, folks, you have read quotations from the official version of how mutual funds received permission to become legal pickpockets. There is nothing erroneous or deceptive in the SEC's strange recounting. But there are just a few things omitted.

Vanguard was the protagonist that first attempted to convince the SEC to allow it to use a portion of shareholder assets to pay for promotional and marketing expenses. And it was a technical quirk in Vanguard's organizational structure that permitted it to get the ground rules changed.

The Vanguard Group is unique among mutual fund sponsors in that it is owned by the funds it manages. Indirectly, the shareholders of Vanguard funds own their own management company. Technically, then, Vanguard is a nonprofit organization, a circumstance that does not apply to the rest of the mutual fund industry. As a result of this legal loophole, Vanguard had no way to fund distribution expenses except to have the shareholders pay for them. From a strict accounting standpoint, that is true—but, one would think, that is Vanguard's problem and not something for the SEC to solve.

Nevertheless, the SEC agreed with Vanguard's position. Incredibly, dispensation was granted giving Vanguard special rights (wrongs?) not available to the rest of the mutual fund industry.

You can just imagine how the rest of the industry reacted.

High-priced lawyers and lobbyists charged into Washington screaming that the SEC had given one fund an unfair, unconstitutional, unreasonable, un-American advantage over all the other funds that pay taxes and have officers who contribute to election campaigns.

They won their point. You got the booby prize.

When Rule 12b-1 was passed, many funds suddenly became very magnanimous. They proudly announced that they were dropping their front-end load charges. In proclaiming this startling news, these funds began to sound like used car dealers. Special! We Will Not Be Undersold! We Will Beat Any Offer!

Imagine, a load fund without a load.

Of course.

Of course, they simply replaced their load charges with 12b-1 charges.

The Keystone Custodian Fund, Series S, was one of the first funds to take advantage of the new regulations. It had been a load fund. Presto! Change-o! It dropped all of its load charges. But it got all of its money back and more, courtesy of the Securities and Exchange Commission.

Under 12b-1, up to $1^1/_4$% of all shareholder investments can be taken every year. $1^1/_4$% every year! The investor is thus paying out much, much more than he would have with the original front-end load. In addition, new investors who sold their shares within four years were now required to pay a redemption fee of up to 4%.

Who needs to charge a load? I have friends in Washington.

Other Fees and Outrages

The 12b-1 charges are only the beginning. There are more additional fees than Tylenol has pills—and you need the extra-strength versions to deal with the headaches they cause.

First, let's talk about the redemption fee, sometimes called the back-end load.

This is a charge levied when you sell your shares. Usually, it works on a sliding scale, so that you pay a larger fee if you redeem your shares within a year and a progressively smaller fee until after six years, when the charge is often dropped. The terms and conditions covering this fee vary widely, and you need to read the prospectus to determine the extent of the charge that will be levied against you.

A redemption fee is like financial alimony. You leave, you pay. If you want out because your fund keeps losing money, the fund does not recognize that as an acceptable excuse, and the fee will be automatically deducted before you receive your money. All funds do not charge a redemption fee, but the practice is becoming increasingly popular.

There is a very odd paragraph in the prospectus for the Liberty High-Income Bond Fund concerning redemption fees. It states:

> Shareholders who purchased shares of the fund with proceeds of a redemption of shares of a mutual fund sold with a sales charge or commission and not distributed by Federated Securities will be charged a redemption fee by the fund distributor of 0.50% for redemptions made within one year of purchase.

What that means is if you sell a load fund that is not part of the Federated family and use the money to buy shares in the Liberty High-Income fund, you will be charged a redemption fee if you sell within a year.

Does anybody understand that? Evidently, the *5-Star Investor Newsletter*, published by Morningstar, doesn't understand it, either. It wrote:

> As the Federated example suggests, one of the worst aspects of miscellaneous fees is that they are often hard to excavate from complicated, jargon-filled prospectuses.

Another particularly nasty fee is the reinvested dividend charge.

Most funds permit you to reinvest your dividends without charge. But not all. Some funds exact a commission if you don't accept distribution in cash and want to reinvest in the form of additional shares.

The maximum charge allowed is 7.25%. But that actually works out to 7.8%. If you get $100, the fund keeps $7.25 and credits your account with $92.75. The $7.25 it took represents 7.8% of the $92.75 that was added to your account.

Sometimes reference to this ridiculous charge is carefully hidden or not carefully explained. The prospectus of the Massachusetts Finance Service Fund reads:

> Dividends will be reinvested in additional full or fractional shares at the public offering price (net asset value) plus a sales charge.

This paragraph does not tell you what the sales charge is. More significant, it does not appear in the early section of the prospectus that covers sales charges. It appears, pages later, under "Distribution Options."

Forbes magazine, referring to charges on reinvested dividends, wrote:

> Paying a load when you buy a fund is bad enough. Why prolong the misery?

The AIM Summit Fund is a particularly vile example of outrageous fees, monstrous contract conditions, and capricious charges that could eat you up alive. To begin, there is a 8.5% front-end load. That is the highest commission charge in the mutual fund industry. Only a handful of funds continue to exact such a frightful charge.

Then, you must contract to make monthly installments for fifteen years—fifteen years, as if you were buying a house and not just investing in a mutual fund.

Okay. Let's say that a moderate investor, in a moment of temporary insanity, agrees to pay $50 a month for 15 years. When he wakes up, finally sober, he has made, say, 19 payments. At this point, his wife—who has carefully refrained from calling him an idiot—quietly suggests that it is time to end this nonsense. Convinced that it is his idea, he finally decides to sell. Thirty-seven percent of his investment will have been eaten up by various charges.

And what do you get for your money in this fund that makes Willie Sutton look like a Boy Scout? Well, certainly, the leading fund of all time? Forbes Honor Roll winner 11 times out of 10?

In 1994 the fund lost money. For the preceding three years, it was in the fourth quintile of its group.

Says Morningstar:

> Most investors already roped into this plan should stick with it. It is very difficult to recommend the fund to anybody else, though.

Every mutual fund in the world gets a management fee, to which it is certainly entitled. But shouldn't there be a limit? After all, that money is coming out of your pocket.

In his book, John Bogle says:

> In 1992, a large equity fund paid a fee of $136,278,000 to its investment advisor for picking stocks, plus a performance fee of $24,965,000 for having picked them well.

That's $161,243,000.

Now, can I use the word "greed" without fear of overstating?

In March 1994 the Putnam High-Yield Advantage Fund sent out a proxy statement seeking a 27% increase in its management fee. The previous year, the fund had reported a 41% after-tax profit.

Frances Stevens of Reno, Nevada, voted no.

A month later, she received a letter from George Putnam, chairman of the Putnam funds. It stated:

> According to our records, you elected to vote against the proposed chances in the management contract. This proposal requires approval by 67% of the shares voted at the shareholder meeting. If that percentage is not

achieved, the meeting will be adjourned until a larger number of shareholders vote their proxies, which, in turn, may end up costing the fund more money for further mailings.

According to *Forbes* magazine, the fund was saying that "we will keep making you poorer until you finally agree to make us richer."

To greedy, may I now add arrogant, grasping, and voracious?

The Value Line family of funds and the Seligman and Putnam funds petitioned their shareholders to increase management fees. Such a request comes in the form of a proxy statement, which, unfortunately, many investors ignore or automatically vote for management, on the theory that Daddy knows best.

These three funds were turning profits of 22% to 59% before they held out their begging cups. After the increases were approved, these margins ballooned to 41% and 67%. Sixty-seven percent profit! Captain Kidd would turn green with envy.

The American Heritage Fund asked shareholders to approve a pay package that raised the annual management fee by two-thirds! It also wanted the shareholders to assume $40,000 in office rent, previously paid by management.

The proxy statement explained that the American Heritage Management Company, the fund's investment advisor, had threatened that, without the increase it

> could not assure the Board it would continue to serve as the Fund's investment advisor.

Pay us two-thirds more or we quit. Some people would call that blackmail. At any rate, the shareholders should have called that bluff. In 1994 the American Heritage Fund was one of the biggest losers of all mutual funds—down 35.3%.

Speaking of greed, how about the case of the then named Shearson Lehman Hutton Multiple Opportunities Portfolio?

When it was launched, it took in $500 million within its first five months. Presumably, this inflow did not come from widows and orphans, as the minimum investment was $100,000.

However, the promised performance turned out to be an empty promise, and investors started heading for the exits in large numbers. Then they learned that they had to pay an exit fee of 3% of net asset value. In addition to this severe charge, Shearson collected management fees and various other expenses that totaled another 3% of net assets. It also collected commissions on all of the fund's trades.

The fund performed so badly that only half of that $500 million in original investments remained in the fund.

Shearson's total income from fees, expenses, and commissions amounted to $53 million.

Mutual funds are the most profitable industry in America.

That is a very sweeping statement. In good years, automobile companies make billions. There have been times when the oil industry was awash with profits. Some of the technology companies have posted profits which are almost embarrassing. In face of that background, what bomb-throwing Communist revolutionary dares to make such a statement?

John Bogle, chairman of Vanguard.

Sorry, but I haven't run out of the list of fees yet. Next is the exchange fee.

This charge is often levied if you want to switch from one fund to another. Some funds allow a certain number of exchanges without charge; others hit you from the git-go. Fidelity recently increased these charges and reduced the number of free exchanges it allows. Other funds will be sure to follow.

If, when you redeem your shares, you want your funds to be wired to your bank account, you will pay a wire redemption charge. (Chances are your bank will also charge you for receiving the money and crediting it to your account.)

Some funds charge an account closeout fee, which is separate and apart from—and in addition to—any back-end load. These funds get you coming and going and—going and going.

There is even an account opening fee. The Blanchard Short-Term Global Income fund charges an account opening fee of $75 if you invest only its opening minimum of $3,000. That amounts to a 2.5% load.

If you arrange with your fund to draw out a given sum at regular intervals, you will often pay a systematic withdrawal plan fee. Conversely, if you arrange to purchase a given number of shares at a given time each month, you will often be charged an automatic investment plan fee.

When you purchase a few shares of a fund and let them sit there without adding to them, many funds will charge you an account minimum fee. (One way to get rich is to take a small amount of money from a great many people. In a ten-year period, mutual fund fee revenues went from $1.2 billion a year to $7.5 billion a year.)

Owners of IRAs are not exempt from these nitpicking expenses. Many funds claim that "extra administrative maintenance" is required for IRAs and gleefully add what they call "plan establishment fees" or "annual maintenance charges."

Fidelity and the Delaware funds charge $15 a year for handling IRA accounts. (Fidelity, however, will waive all IRA maintenance charges if there is a minimum balance kept as the total of your Fidelity accounts.) Merrill Lynch charges $100 a year, just to "maintain" an account, but exactly what it means by the term "maintain" is not clear. The root of the word "maintain" derives from Middle English and means "to hold in the hand."

Merrill Lynch's hand, of course.

New Classes of Shares

Some mutual fund promoters have come up with a gimmick that insults the intelligence of the average investor, adds confusion to an already difficult subject, and falls just short of being a scam.

These funds have created four different classes of mutual fund shares: A, B, C, and D.

There is absolutely no difference in the earning power of these shares—the only difference is how they charge fees and other expenses.

If your broker or banker or investment planner tells you with the golden tones of a snake oil promoter that "I want you to have Class A shares," you might naturally conclude that these are the best shares available. Certainly, they must have something that the other shares don't have.

A load.

If you buy Class A shares, the individual selling them to you gets his commission right off the top.

Class B shares have no front-end load.

Hold your applause. In this case, the fund gets its money by exacting a 12b-1 charge, plus a back-end charge that starts at 4%. The 12b-1 fee stays, usually for six years, after which the fund, with its usual generosity, reduces a percentage of the charge.

Class C shares just take a 1% annual fee. Forever.

Class D shares charge a 1% front-end load and an annual 12b-1 fee of .50%.

I explained all this to a Nobel Prize winner; he burst into tears.

A simple example will demonstrate how difficult it is to figure out which are the best shares to purchase.

You have $10,000 to invest, and you are going to let it stay in the fund for 25 years. If your annual return is 10% before load and 12b-1 charges, is A better than B, C worse than D, C the same as A, or None of the Above?

The answer is: A is better than B.

At the end of 25 years, assuming an annual return of 10%, Class A shares would have grown to $102,930. B shares would have turned into $91,314; C shares, $86,231; and D shares, $91,314.

If, however, you redeemed your shares after just five years,

Class A shares would have been your worst choice. In that circumstance, Class D shares would have been the best option.

Madness.

Why were all these classifications created in the first place? There are two answers: (e) and (f).

(e) This answer will be supplied by your broker, banker, or financial planner, who will say that it was done to give the investor more options. If an investor expects to own the fund for a long time, this fairy tale goes, he should pay the commission right away; over a long period of time, the load should represent a smaller percentage than if he had to pay a set amount each and every year. If, however, the investor is in for the short term, he can avoid the big front-end load by buying Class B or C shares.

(f) With four classes of shares, the salesperson has four separate shots at you. "You are dead set against a front-end load? Fine. I happen to have here these lovely Class B or C shares which have no front-end load." Or "You were told not to buy any fund with a 12b-1 charge? I agree with you—let's buy Class A shares—there is absolutely no 12b-1 fee involved."

Furthermore, presenting all these options makes the salesperson look good. He knows all the answers. Aren't you glad you are in the hands of such a wise man?

Worry not about the salesperson who sells you shares without a front-end load. He still gets his commission—it just comes out of the 12b-1 charges.

Don Lee is a certified financial planner and a teacher at Harvard. He said: "The different classes of shares are confusing to me, a financial professional."

Added Jon Fossel, chairman of Oppenheimer Management: "Buying a fund may be like buying a car—you'll worry that you are paying the sticker price while someone else is getting a better deal."

I lied. There are really three answers:

(g) As Nancy Reagan suggested, "Just say no."

I hate to do this to you, but there are yet more new classes of shares, each created by an individual fund for its own impossible-to-understand reasons.

The Nations Fund now has class N shares. These are just Class B shares under another name. Class N shares have a back-end load of 4.5%, if redeemed within a year. After that, the charge declines gradually and is eliminated after six years. But you just knew that there would be some other goodies involved. Class N shares include an annual "administrative fee" of 0.25% and an annual "sales support" fee of 0.75%. There is no additional charge for laughing.

The Quantitative fund group now has O class shares. Oh, they include an annual 12b-1 fee and a 1% redemption charge, no matter how long you keep the shares.

Nuveen has R shares. Any shares you once held in Nuveen funds were automatically converted to R shares, whether you liked it or not, because they didn't ask you. Now, if you reinvest your dividends or capital distribution into new shares, you must buy Class A or Class C shares with that money. And you pay a sales load on your dividends and capital distribution. Whether you like it or not.

Insanity.

You may not pass Go. Park Place and Boardwalk are equal to two Class B shares, unless you invest in the Telephone Company or in Utilities, which are each worth one D share and a fifth of an A share. Wouldn't you be better off in Jail?

Expenses

Expenses are another matter. Funds have expenses—and they are deducted from the net asset value. The higher the expense ratio, the less money you take home.

Come on—we're talking about the difference of a half percent or a percent—why am I making a federal case here?

The difference between 1% and 2% in a fund's expenses can make a significant difference, even to the small investor. If you were to invest just $10,000, and assuming a 10% annual return, in ten years that extra 1% would have reduced your return by more than $2,250.

How can a few lousy basis points make an important difference in a fund's overall performance?

The Institute for Econometric Research looked into that question and came up with some startling results:

Annual Expenses	5-Year Fund Performance
0.5 to 1%	41%
1% to 2%	37%
2% or more	16%

Funds in the first category, with the lowest expense ratios, averaged a 41% return over the five years of this study. Funds in the third category, with the highest expense ratio, averaged a 16% return over the same period.

It will come as no great surprise to you that the study also proved that the higher the 12b-1 charge, the lower the average performance:

Annual 12b-1 fees	5-Year Fund Performance
Less than 0.5%	34%
1% or more	23%

John Markese, president of the American Association of Individual Investors, said:

> All you know with any certainty is the future expense ratio, and so if it's above normal, you have to figure it's going to affect your return over time. No fund manager stays above his peer group for very long, so expense ratios come back to haunt you in the long run.

Sheldon Jacobs, publisher of *The No-Load Fund Investor*, did some research, over a five-year period, of funds that had an expense ratio of 2% or higher. He discovered that 45% of those funds fell into the bottom quintile of all mutual fund performers.

He added:

> If expense ratios had no impact at all, the higher-ratio funds would be distributed evenly in terms of performance. Obviously, that is not the case.

And Don Phillips, publisher of the *Morningstar Mutual Fund Reports,* added:

> Investors are going to have to spend more time looking at these costs. No service has infinite value. At some point, the costs can and will outweigh the benefits.

But there is a way to avoid the high expense funds.

Buy Vanguard funds.

Vanguard is the low-cost champ. The average asset-weighted annual expense ratio for Vanguard's equity fund is a miserly 0.37%—about half that of its nearest competitor. Expenses of the average non-Vanguard fund through 1994 were 1.08%. (More than 150 funds have expense ratios of 2.5% or higher—they should be avoided like the plague.)

Fidelity, the largest family of funds, was 11th out of 41 fund families in descending order of average fund expenses. The two highest—Keystone and G.T. Global.

In bond funds, Vanguard was also the lowest, with a tight-fisted 0.24 expense ratio. Fidelity was sixth-lowest, but its expense ratio in this category was double that of Vanguard. The two highest? Pilgrim, at 1.66%, and Keystone, at 1.72%.

Let's say you are considering the investment of $10,000 in one of three funds. You expect a 10% annual return over the next 25 years.

Fund A has a 0.5 expense ratio—actually slightly higher than the average Vanguard equity fund.

Fund B has a 1.5% expense ratio—just a touch above average.

Fund C has a 2.5% expense ratio.

How much more money would you make with Fund A as opposed to Fund C?

70% more!

That is not a typographical error. Seventy percent more. The difference between Fund A and Fund C in real money is $35,701. With a $10,000 initial investment, over the indicated period, you would earn $35,701 more with Fund A than with Fund C.

After deducting expenses, Fund A nets 9.58% a year, which develops $20,000 worth of extra compound earnings, for a total of $86,684. The same computation for Fund C produces a 7.5% return, which works out to a cumulative profit of $50,983. The difference is $35,701.

I must make clear that I have not written this book in order to hawk Vanguard funds. It has some funds which do very well; it has some funds which do, well, not so well. All I am saying is that it has the lowest average expense ratio of any family of funds.

I hope I have made clear that a seemingly small difference in annual expense ratios can make a very big difference in your total return.

An annual expense ratio over 1.50 is very high; over 2.00 is ridiculous; over 2.50 is absurd. Here is a list of funds whose 1994 annual expense ratio was 3.00% or higher:

Alliance New Europe B	3.02%
American Capitalization World Growth Equity	3.21%
Atlanta Growth	4.82%
Blanchard American Equity	3.00%
Bull & Bear U.S. Overseas	3.55%
Captstone Nikko Japan	4.26%
Centura Growth	3.20%
Eaton Golden Northern Resources	3.15%
44 Wall Street Equity	5.01%
Keystone Global Opportunity	3.04%
Merrill Lynch Global Conv.	3.26%
Pilgrim Global Shares	3.10%

Prudent Speculator	4.41%
Prudential Global Natural Resources	3.18%
Smith Barney Metals	3.00%
Steadman American Industry	12.66%
Steadman Associate	5.79%
Steadman Investment	7.78%
Steadman Technology and Growth	13.33%

In February 1993 a *Forbes* magazine article titled "Fee Madness" observed:

> How do you, the investor, know whether you are paying too much for a manager's services? Here's a definition of a bad buy: a fund that cost 2% a year for the time you hold it. Our definition of a really bad buy: a fund that eats away 3% of your money each year.
> In the merely bad category are scores of funds with expenses over 2%. What's so bad about a 2% fee for professional management in a market that seems to be shooting up 15% a year? Just the fact that you can't count on that 15% very long. Remember, you will still be nicked that 2% if the fund loses money for you.
> A bad stock fund, then, is fixing to take a third of the real money you can expect to earn on your investment. Or to aggravate any losses the fund may incur in bad markets.

Ninety-five percent of the funds on the list have front-end loads. One hundred percent of them have expense ratios which are a serious drag on performance and profitability. Yet, together, they have thousands upon thousands of investors. Lethargy? Unfounded trust in stockbrokers? A too-simple belief that, eventually, everything goes up in the stock market and a few expense fractions are not worth worrying about?

It will pay you to worry just a little bit.

Soft Dollars

When are expenses not expenses? How can a mutual fund cost you money by reducing its expenses?

Those questions are not as silly as they sound.

Ever hear of "soft dollars"?

A fund gives a lot of business to brokerage houses for executing its trades. The brokerage house then "repays" the fund for this largesse by buying it a new computer system, doing special research projects, or upgrading its telephone system, to select just a few examples of this pervasive practice. The money used by the brokers to pay for these items is called "soft dollars."

This business of scratching each other's back is certainly crooked and should be objected to on ethical grounds. But, being practical, why should an investor complain? His fund is saving money by not having the expense of that new computer system or that telephone upgrade. These savings go right to the bottom line and should result in increased profits.

The fund is happy—it saved money. The broker is happy—he is getting a lot of business and returning only a very small part of his profits. And the investor, as indicated, should be very happy if his fund is reducing its expenses.

Well, for one, the Securities and Exchange Commission is not happy.

Said SEC chairman Arthur Levitt:

> Advisers may cause their clients to pay excessive commission rates, or may overtrade their clients' accounts simply to satisfy soft-dollar obligations. Soft-dollar arrangements may also result in inferior executions when advisers direct trades to the wrong broker to satisfy soft-dollar obligations.

The SEC has proposed a rule that would require funds to be forthcoming about what services they really get in exchange for commission dollars.

There is another word for soft-dollar transactions: graft.

Brokerage firms have been known to provide vacation trips for portfolio managers, and the word is all over the Street that enterprising managers have received nonbusiness-related gifts, including expensive clothing and even more expensive cars.

Who do you think pays for all this in the end? You do, of course. As the SEC has indicated, this matter seems to be getting out of hand.

As investors, we cannot just tsk! tsk! and shrug our shoulders. The least you can do is write to your fund and express your displeasure. Write to Chairman Levitt and let him know he has your support.

It may not help—but you will feel better.

Investors of the world, arise! You have nothing to lose but your gains.

Four

Claims! Claims! Claims!

Many Mutual Funds Are Guilty of Misleading Advertising, Purposeful Omissions, Selective Performance Ratings, And Other Fancy Falsehoods

"Lord, Lord, how this world is given to lying."
—from *King Henry IV* by William Shakespeare

In 1994, the Templeton Global Fund advertised that it was the leading global fund over a 30-year period.

True.

What it failed to note was that it was the only global fund with a 30-year record.

Would you classify that as:

57

   A. A misleading half-truth.
   B. A shameful evasion of the truth.
   C. An outright lie.
   D. All of the above.

It is also symbolic of the let-'em-eat-cake, never-give-a-sucker-an-even-break attitude of some (many?) mutual funds. A question leaps disturbingly to mind: if these funds are devious and unethical in their advertising, does this posture permeate their entire operations? In short, are you in a den of thieves?

Answer: sometimes.

Take the case of the advertising by the Pilgrim Fund which resulted in a threatened lawsuit and charges that the ads were "libelous," showed "reckless disregard," and were "defamatory."

Pilgrim ran an advertisement in which it listed five of its mutual funds and gave each of them a number, 1 through 5. According to *The New York Times,* the advertisement

> "clearly gave the impression that the five funds shown
> had commanded the top five spots in a category."

Minor problem: It was not true.

The advertisement stated that the performance was "in its category" but provided absolutely no information as to which category, or who had decided which categories these funds properly belonged to.

More pointed, also according to *The New York Times,* which quoted the Lipper Analytical Service, the truth was that these funds ranked third, seventh, thirteenth, fourteenth, and fifteenth in their properly assigned categories.

Said Don Phillips, publisher of *Morningstar:*

> That Pilgrim could twist its often poor performance re-
> cord to create marketing material that makes it look
> like the industry's most successful manager presents an

important lesson in the use and abuse of statistics in the fund industry today.

Pilgrim sued Morningstar. The case was thrown out of court. All of the "leading" funds mentioned in the advertisement then suffered grievous losses, and the company was eventually sold.

The T. Rowe Price Science and Technology fund advertised that it "is ranked #1 out of 15 science and technology funds since its inception (9/30/87 through 9/30/94)."

Correct. But that was only because it had a great year in 1991, which was preceded by a losing year and followed by a catastrophic year when the fund dropped 70% below its total return for 1991. The headline of its advertisement screamed: "Ranked #1 In High Tech." Incredible. In the tiny print at the bottom of the advertisement, the fund itself admitted that, over a five-year period, it ranked fifth out of 15 such funds and, for the one-year period, twelfth out of 22.

As John Keefe, of Keefe Worldwide Information, said: "The large print giveth and the small print taketh away."

The Securities and Exchange Commission cannot be expected to review every mutual fund advertisement. The newspapers and magazines in which the advertisements appear cannot be expected to do the research necessary to determine their truthfulness. As a result, some funds can say almost anything they please. Many year later, the SEC may make them sit in the corner during recess.

Some funds emphasize their high yields in their advertising. But, as *Business Week* magazine pointed out:

> Funds can play around with expense charges, temporarily absorbing some fees, to increase yield. But once the fees are reinstated, the yield will fall.

Exaggerated claims, misleading statements, playing fast and loose with the books—is this the hallowed bastion of American capitalism or some sleazy used-car dealer?

You think some funds don't deliberately mislead? Talk to New York City's Consumer Affairs Department. It charged the Dreyfus Growth and Income Fund with precisely that: deceptive advertising.

In its brochure, the Dreyfus fund boasted that it did not invest in junk bonds. In its prospectus, however, it stated that it can invest in "convertible securities that can be below investment grade."

"Junk!" said Consumer Affairs.

If "convertible securities below investment grade" are not junk, then will somebody please tell me and Michael Milken exactly what junk is? Perhaps the answer is that junk is what Dreyfus put in its advertisements.

Everybody Is #1

There were three mutual fund advertisements in the *The New York Times* on December 4, 1994.

The Robertson Stephens Value and Growth Fund said that it was:

#1 out of 260 small growth funds.

Immediately next to it was an advertisement for the Montgomery Fund which said it was the:

#1 performer among 452 growth funds.

On a preceding page, there was an advertisement for the Kaufmann Fund which said it was the:

#1 performing fund since the market low of 1987.

Strangely enough, they are all telling the truth.

Well, sort of.

The Robertson Stephens fund invests primarily in small

capitalization companies. The Montgomery Fund invests in both small and large capitalization companies. Therefore, says Robertson Stephens, it cannot be compared with Montgomery.

Baloney.

(I would use a stronger word but Senator Helms may read this book.)

Morningstar does not even recognize the category of "small growth funds" claimed by Robertson Stephens. The fund made it up.

I love the comment of Richard Schilffarth, a former E. F. Hutton broker. He said: "I interviewed 800 money managers, and I never found one who was in the bottom half."

In early 1993, I received a solicitation from the Fundamental U.S. Government Strategic Income Fund. It consisted of a double-faced postcard, in color, with a tear-off return card. The front of the card said:

Playing It Safe Was Never So Rewarding.

The copy on the other side of the card said:

Introducing a flexible new investment designed to provide high current yields plus the maximum safety of U.S. Government securities.

"Maximum safety" and "U.S. Government Securities" were underlined.

The body of the card contained such phrases as ". . . for conservative investors," "high yields and maximum safety," "AAA quality portfolio," and "more price stability than ordinary long-term funds."

In addition, the magic words were there: U.S. Government Income Fund. How bad could it be?

Morningstar does not report on this fund, so, late in 1994, I called John Rekenthaler, the editor, and asked him how this "conservative fund" offering "high yields and maximum safety" had done. He replied:

"Absymal. Worse than absymal. For 1994, it was down 25.1%."

The Investment Company Institute speaks for the mutual fund industry. It is, in fact, the industry's lobbyist and is financed by contributions from mutual funds. In early 1995, I talked to Erick Kantor, vice president for public information and marketing. He said: "We are a regulated industry. All mutual fund advertising must live up to accepted standards."

Sure.

Charles Schwab ran an advertisement in *The Wall Street Journal* (November 28, 1994) in which it showed the performance record for some of the funds it has available for sale.

One of those funds is Yacktman—and Schwab showed an annualized return for it of 16.9%. Not bad.

But not true, either. In fact, it never happened.

This fund started in mid-1992 and, according to Morningstar, showed a 4.72% gain for the remainder of that year. For 1993, Morningstar reported that it lost 6.58%. Through November 1994—when the Schwab advertisement appeared—it was up all of 0.53%.

Certainly, Mr. Kantor, the mutual fund industry is regulated. And, certainly, you did say that all mutual fund advertising must live up to accepted standards.

And, certainly, this example might prove to have been an honest mistake.

Wanna bet?

On February 1, 1995, Warburg Pincus ran an advertisement in *The Wall Street Journal.* It claimed:

In a tough market, the performance of Warburg Pincus Growth and Income Fund has been tough to beat.

That depends upon who's counting and what they count.

In the three-year period from 1991 through 1993, six other growth and income funds far surpassed the Warburg Pincus cumulative record. The Oppenheimer fund, in this category, more than doubled the Warburg Pincus return over those three years, with a plus 132.84% record, compared to the Warburg Pincus cumulative return over the same period of plus 59.21%.

The year 1992 was, indeed, a tough market for growth and income funds, and the Warburg Pincus total return fell to plus 9.13% after some strong previous years. However, in the same year, the Oppenheimer Growth and Income Fund showed a 31.08% return. Other growth and income funds also beat Warburg Pincus: Mutual Qualified was up 28.70%; Mutual Beacon, up 22.92%; and Main Stay, up 20.71%.

Warburg Pincus Growth and Income is a fine fund, with strong management and an outstanding record. Why does it have to play games with its numbers?

The Strong International Stock Fund had a four-color advertisement on the back cover of the December 1994 issue of *Mutual Funds* magazine.

The advertisement had a prominent chart which showed the eight countries whose stock markets outperformed those of the United States over a ten-year period. More than half of this fund's investments are in five foreign countries—Australia, Great Britain, Japan, Sweden, and New Zealand. None of its money is in any of the three countries (Hong Kong, Switzerland, and France) that lead the chart as having the best performing stock markets compared with the NYSE.

This is an advertising technique which should be labeled Innocence by Association. The chart has absolutely nothing to do with the performance of this fund. Nevertheless, it hopes you will send in your money, even though the fund wasn't smart enough to put a preponderance of its investments in the foreign stock markets that went up the most.

By the way, the Strong International Fund was weak in 1994. It lost money for the year.

A Strong fund was also involved in some fancy footwork with its advertisement in *The New York Times* on January 3, 1995, which reached a new height of absurdity in the race to be #1. Its headline read: "#1 Yielding Money Market Fund."

The body copy proclaimed that it was the #1 fund "for the 7-day period ended 12-20-94."

Seven days! I fully expect to see an advertisement that claims that a fund was #1 on a given Tuesday between 11:32 A.M. and 12:09 P.M.

There was a small line at the bottom of this advertisement which stated: "Performance is historical."

It should have said: Performance is hysterical.

On January 19, 1995, two money market funds ran advertisements in *The Wall Street Journal,* each claiming to be #1. (Will this insanity never stop?)

Dreyfus said that its Basic U.S. Government Money Market fund was:

> Ranked #1 of the 100 money market funds in the U.S. Government and Agencies Category as reported in IBC/Donoghue's Money Fund Report for the 7-day period ended 1/10/95.

The headline of the Strong Money Market Fund advertisement read: "#1 Yielding Money Fund."

The copy stated:

> For the 7 days ended 1-10-95, the Strong Money Market Fund ranked #1 for yield among the 206 General Purpose money funds tracked by the Money Fund Report, a service of IBC/Donoghue.

Same source, same time period, yet we have two funds each claiming to be #1.

But that's not the half of it.

By another of those fascinating coincidences, on that very same day the *Journal* listed the top 15 performers in money market funds.

Neither the Dreyfus fund nor the Strong fund was included in the top 15!

The winner was the Benham Prime Money Market Fund.

On January 3, 1995, Robertson Stephens had an advertisement in *The Wall Street Journal* for its Emerging Growth Fund. It displayed, in very large type, the fund's average annual return since inception, its five-year average annual return, and its one-year return.

The figure for the one-year return was plus 16%.

Which year?

It certainly wasn't 1994 because in the very same issue *The Wall Street Journal* printed the one-year return for all mutual funds, and the figure given for the Robertson Stephens Emerging Growth Fund was:

9.5%.

Could the reference have been to 1993? No. In that year, its return was 7.22%.

How about 1992? Hardly. That year its total return was minus 2.55%.

Morningstar has tracked this fund since 1987. There was never a calendar year when it showed a 16.0% return.

Robertson Stevens, permit me to ask you a question. Do you believe in the truth, the whole truth and nothing but the truth?

The answer may be found in the Hertz television commercial: Not exactly.

"Selective" Performance Records

The Merrill Lynch advertisement in *The Wall Street Journal* (January 6, 1995) is a horrendous example of purposeful omissions, erroneous information, and the deliberate selection of certain time periods to make the fund look better than the facts warranted.

One of the funds highlighted in the advertisement was Merrill Lynch's Eurofund, for which its claims read:

#1 European Regional Fund
5 years 8.00%. 1 Year 10.22%

Morningstar lists 10 other funds in its general "Europe" category. Six of these 10 funds did not exist five years ago. Merrill Lynch told the narrow truth—it beat four other funds.

However, in a comparison of annualized returns over a three-year period, the Merrill Lynch Eurofund came in not first, not second, not third, but fourth. On a one-year basis—1994—it came in seventh.

The most amazing thing in this advertisement, however, is the claim that the fund had a one-year return of 10.22%.

This particular issue of *The Wall Street Journal* has a chart showing the one, three, and five-year returns for all funds. Right there, on the preceding page, is the one-year return for the Merrill Lynch Eurofund:

4.3%.

Deceptive advertising by mutual funds can fool some of the people some of the time, but a deceptive name of a mutual fund can fool most of the people most of the time.

I am referring to funds with the words "United States Government" in their names.

Take the Abbott U.S. Government Securities Fund. That certainly sounds like a hidebound, conservative fund that invests only in United States Treasury bills and notes and other financial instruments backed by the full faith and credit of the United States government.

Quite the contrary. In 1944, only 12% of its portfolio was in U.S. Treasuries. The remainder was in mortgage-backed securities. Could have fooled me.

More bizarre is the Value Line U.S. Government Securities Fund. Seventy-three percent of its holdings were in collateralized mortgage obligations, not U.S. Treasury paper.

Said Morningstar:

> The fund's performance is particularly galling because the fund has put itself forth as a relatively conservative intermediate-term fund.

The Piper Jaffrey Institutional Government fund plunged 28% in 1994.

Could happen to anybody. Funds go up, funds go down. A 28% loss is pretty rough, but lots of funds lost lots of money in 1994.

The problem for Piper Jaffrey was not only the loss, but also the fact that it had misrepresented the risk of the fund. Its name says "Institutional Government," and it was marketed as an especially low-risk investment. In actuality, its money was mostly in complex securities backed by home mortgages.

A series of class action suits was instituted against the firm. Piper Jaffrey agreed to pay $70 million to settle the suits.

The firm still faces suits seeking to redress losses on several other funds it managed, and it has also been sued by stockholders who claim that Piper Jaffrey made misleading statements that artificially inflated the company's stock price.

Kiplinger's Personal Finance magazine wrote:

> Most of the volatile, unpredictable derivative securities that went awry in 1994 were derived from mortgage securities. In other words, you can buy shares in a fund with "government income" in its name in anticipation of calm sailing and end up in the gale of a financial hurricane.

"The Check Is in the Mail"

Evelyn Ringold—no relation—owns what for her is a substantial number of shares in the Lindner Dividend Fund. She is a careful record keeper and depends upon these dividends to fill specific holes in her budget.

The end-of-the-year payment for this fund was declared on December 30, 1994, and was due to be received by the shareholders during the first week of January 1995.

It did not arrive.

Evelyn was familiar with all the horror stories about the slow-moving post office, so she decided to allow a whole additional week before she took action. She called the fund on Monday, January 16, two weeks after the payment was due. She was told that there had been an unavoidable delay but that the checks had been sent out on the previous Friday, the 13th of January.

When the check still hadn't arrived by the middle of the next week—January 18—she called again. This time, she was told that the checks had absolutely, positively, been mailed the day before—January 17, changing the previous story, which had assured her the money was sent out on the 13th.

The check finally arrived on January 23.

Which raises an interesting question: was this just a general snafu or a deliberate attempt by the Lindner fund to delay the distribution of its dividend?

Why would a prestigious fund like Lindner do a terrible thing like that? While there is no hard evidence that the fund was at fault (try proving it), had the action been deliberate, Lindner would have profited considerably by retaining its dividend for the three weeks involved.

Have you any idea of the total amount of money a large dividend fund pays out at the end of the year? Three weeks' additional interest accruing to the fund is not an insignificant sum. The checks were not delayed by the post office, as the postmark clearly indicated.

Anybody got any better ideas?

Let the record in this matter clearly show yet another example where dividends from a large fund were mysteriously delayed. Checks from a Franklin fund were received by shareholders in April. The envelopes were postmarked February.

Where had they been for two months? Sixty days a lot of interest makes.

Bruce Brown, writing in the April 1995 issue of *Kiplinger's Personal Finance* magazine, described his strange experience with the T. Rowe Price Short-Term Bond Fund. For some unexplained reason, this fund sends two checks when an account is closed—one for the principal involved, a second for the interest that has accrued. The money for the principal arrived promptly; the check for the interest did not.

Brown called and was told the blackest of white lies—the check is in the mail. It wasn't.

He called again.

Finally, the check arrived—17 days after it was due. From the time he closed the account until the check was written, the fund dropped 3 cents a share. That amount was deducted from his final payment.

Brown also tells the sad story about Larry Berkowitz, of Fort Myers, Florida. He had $200,000 in a Fidelity fund which he closed out.

He received his money—three weeks later.

The accounts payable departments of all of these funds are computerized. There is no excuse for failure to make payments promptly.

Unless it is an organized slowdown.

Watch out for deceptive advertising. Watch out for false claims. Watch out for "selective" performance ratings. Watch out for funds that do not remit your money promptly.

Watch out!

Five

There Are More Than 6,000 Mutual Funds—How Do You Pick the Right One for You?

The First Thing to Do: Understand the Differences Between Them.

"The difficulty in life is choice."

—George Moore

This chapter is going to be very dull.

It will try to explain the objectives and strategies of various types of funds. You will love it—there's a yawn every minute.

Do you know the difference between a growth fund and a growth and income fund? Do you understand how an index

71

fund works? Can you, right this minute, explain the difference between a high-yield corporate bond fund, a general corporate bond fund, and a high-quality corporate bond fund? Are you sure? How about a government bond as opposed to a treasury bond fund?

Try taking this chapter in small doses—a couple of pages, a good nap, some mild exercise, even a cold shower.

Do you really want to make money with mutual funds?

Then, dammit, read the chapter.

Aggressive Growth Funds

Aggressive growth funds, by accepted definition, invest in stocks that are not in the mainstream; in sectors of the economy that may be out of favor; in smaller, emerging companies; in industries that have fallen on hard times; and in volatile issues that are reminiscent of the old discredited go-go years.

Some do. Some don't.

The term "aggressive growth" is misleading and misunderstood. It does not mean that these funds are all high rollers, gambling on lost gold mines, on penny stocks, or on bankrupt companies whose CEOs are spending time in jail for fraud.

Enterprise Capital Appreciation is an aggressive growth fund, and its two leading investments are Motorola and Microsoft. Seligman Capital is an aggressive growth fund, and its heaviest investments are in Home Depot, Microsoft, Motorola, and the Interpublic Group. AIM Constellation is an aggressive growth fund, and its leading holdings are Compaq and Intel. As a group, aggressive growth funds own such "nonmainstream" stocks as Ford, AT&T, Johnson & Johnson, Volvo, and Toyota.

The objective of aggressive growth funds is long-term capital appreciation. They do invest in smaller capitalized companies, wherever they can find the promise of above-average earnings growth. They do buy stocks that they believe are underpriced and ignored by Wall Street. They do place big bets on companies with new products and services, on promising technological developments, even on floundering companies where new management offers the hope for a dramatic turnaround. And some aggressive growth funds use adventurous investing techniques, including margined portfolios, options, and short selling.

That involves risk.

Aggressive growth funds are easily the most volatile of all diversified equity funds. They also—sometimes—produce extraordinary results.

Most aggressive growth funds are not for the faint of heart. Some of them produce amazing gains and then spectacular losses.

Morningstar's comment on the ABT Emerging Growth Fund: "It's definitely not for the queasy, but those who can stomach its risks may be amply rewarded."

The American Heritage Fund, an aggressive growth fund managed by the well-known Heike Thiene, was among 1994's biggest losers, ending the year minus 35.3%. In 1991 it gained 96.04%.

Like all other equity investments, you bets your money and you takes your chances. For investors with some extra money they can afford to lose, aggressive growth funds offer an unusual opportunity to hit the jackpot. Conservative investors should be warned that aggressive growth funds can be dangerous to their wealth.

Asset Allocation Funds

Asset allocation funds divide their assets between stocks and bonds. They try to change the mix as market conditions vary. The concept, in very general terms, is that if stocks go down, the income from bonds will make up the losses. These funds tend to spread the investment risk over a wide spectrum, often resulting in just moderate returns. They also tend to perform better in down markets than many other fund groups.

There is, however, a very wide divergence in their investing styles—and in the results. Some of them like to overweight international funds, which can get risky; others, more conservative, keep a greater percentage of their money in bonds and other fixed-income securities.

Blanchard Global Growth and Managers Global Growth Opportunity, for example, are heavy international investors. Crabbe Hudson Asset Allocation and Connecticut Mutual Total Return own no international stocks.

Generally, asset allocation funds try to strike a happy balance between stocks and bonds, which usually (not always) behave in opposition to each other, thus smoothing what might otherwise be a bumpy ride.

As Michael Strathearn, comanager of the Connecticut Mutual Total Return Fund, said: "We don't swing for the fences."

A proper balance of stocks and bonds makes sense. Bonds usually return principal in a timely fashion and provide a known return, even though they are vulnerable to rising interest rates. Stocks, if the portfolio manager is smart (and lucky), can provide higher returns over time, particularly the sedate issues favored by this group. The question is: how good is the portfolio manager in maintaining his balance?

As a group, asset allocation funds rarely yield spectacular returns, but they do wind up consistently near the average of most equity funds. If you are conservative—but not all that conservative—your risk/reward ratio could be quite rewarding in an asset allocation fund.

Balanced Funds

It is often difficult to tell the difference between balanced funds and asset allocation funds because they both make up their portfolios with a mixture of stocks, bonds, and fixed securities.

Balanced funds tend to be a little riskier because more than 50% of their assets is usually in stocks and the mix is not changed as often. Slightly more risk should produce slightly more gain.

It hasn't.

In the years since 1983, balanced funds, as a group, have rarely outperformed the S&P 500. In stormy 1987 the S&P 500 digested Black Monday and ended the year up 5.26%. Balanced funds managed only a 1.85% gain.

1994 was a particularly bad year for balanced funds as they were hit by a double whammy. Their bond positions suffered from rising interest rates; in addition, most of them had large positions in utilities and financial stocks, which lost ground through most of the year.

Balanced funds fall into various subgroups. Some, like Vanguard's Wellington fund, usually hold a mix of 60% stocks and 40% bonds. In the same family, however, Vanguard's Wellesley fund is more income-oriented and favors bonds over stocks.

Balanced funds were among the first mutual funds to be organized in the United States. It wasn't long, however, before some of them became disorganized as investors found few rewards from their basic concept. The Scudder Stevens and Clark Balanced Fund changed its name to Scudder Income and completely dropped the "balanced" strategy. The SteinRoe Farnham Balanced Fund also left the flock, becoming the SteinRoe Total Return Fund. Morningstar no longer lists it as a balanced fund. This small slice of history, however, should not give you the wrong impression—there are some excellent balanced funds with great records and great prospects.

In theory, balanced funds are designed to protect you against yourself. If you are financially timid, you can put your money into Treasury bills and certificates of deposit where you are assured safety but have no protection from the ravages of inflation. With balanced funds, you can seek capital gains and still have the cushion of the bond portion to reduce any damage.

Equity Income Funds

Equity income funds seek current income. They are primarily interested in dividend and short-term growth, with long-range capital appreciation a secondary consideration.

Of the 30 equity income funds listed by Morningstar, 29 have risk ratings of Low or Below Average. As a group, they are among the most conservative of all equity funds.

Equity income funds invest heavily in stocks with strong dividend-paying records—the three largest holdings of the group are Philip Morris, General Electric, and American Express. Utility stocks make up 15% of the group's investments, with significant additional holdings in fixed-income securities.

Low or Below Average risk does not mean no risk. Equity income funds are adversely affected by rapidly rising interest rates, just like most other funds. In 1993, the IDS Diversified Equity Income Fund had a profit of 24.9%; in 1994, it lost 2.4%.

As a group, the history of equity income funds is just what you might expect—not very exciting, but usually respectable, in keeping with its generally reduced level of risk. In 1992 the group had a 9.14% gain; in 1993, a 13.5% advance. In 1994, in a generally down market, it had an almost unnoticeable loss.

Equity income funds provide a return competitive to bond funds while also offering a small opportunity for capital appreciation. Reasonably safe, reasonably sure—a reasonable selection for the conservative investor.

Growth Funds

Growth funds seek capital appreciation rather than dividends and invest mostly in well-established, substantial companies. The group's portfolio profile is almost a duplicate of the Dow, with heavy investments in General Electric, Philip Morris, IBM, Sears, and Motorola. No roulette players or long-odds horse betters here.

A look at the growth funds that have earned Morningstar's 5-star rating reveals a sameness that makes them appear to be clones of each other.

The leading holdings of the Magellan Fund are Motorola and Oracle Systems. The leading holdings of the Berger 100 Fund are Motorola and Oracle Systems. The heaviest investments of the John Hancock Growth Fund are Motorola and Mc-Donald's; the heaviest investments of the IAI Regional Fund are Motorola and McDonald's. Growth funds own a $1.5 billion worth of Intel and $1.3 billion worth of IBM.

So, how have they done?

As a group, not spectacularly, not disastrously. In 1991, when other funds heavy in technology and health stocks were producing 50% to 75% gains, growth funds managed a 36% profit. In 1992, when financial funds showed a 35.8% gain, growth funds just made it to the plus side with a 8.43% increase. In 1993, international stocks racked up 40.2% profits, growth funds only 11.7%. And 1994 was a mixed bag—some growth funds were caught in the general down trend; others managed surprisingly healthy gains. Fidelity's Magellan lost 1.8%, but its Blue Chip Fund was up 9.8%. Guardian Park Avenue, a previous longtime resident on the *Forbes* Honor Roll, lost 1.4%; Longleaf Partners gained 17.1%.

Growth funds are America. If you believe that, in the long run, this country will grow and prosper, then you certainly need to own the Coca Colas, General Electrics, and AT&Ts of this world. Long-term investors who are trying to build a nest egg for retirement could not make a better choice.

Growth and Income Funds

Growth and income funds try to give you the best of both worlds—accelerating growth and a steady flow of dividends.

As a group, however, they have beaten the S&P 500 only twice in the last 12 years, once by just 0.65%. For nine straight years, from 1983 to 1991, the group underperformed that index.

The obvious attraction of these funds is that they are supposed to deliver capital appreciation plus yield. Unfortunately, the typical growth and income fund has failed to produce a yield better than—or even competitive with—the yield of the S&P 500. But don't let that word "typical" fool you. Like every other mutual fund investment, the outcome depends upon which fund you select. And those dividends do tend to cushion market volatility.

Never underestimate the power of dividends.

In the 15-year period from 1988 through the end of 1993, the S&P 500 went from 96 to 466, a 370-point increase, not counting dividends. If reinvested dividends had been included, the index would have made a leap to 858—a 793% increase.

If aggressive growth funds make you nervous and if balanced funds are too stodgy for your taste, picking the right growth and income fund could be the ideal middle ground.

Love those dividends.

Health Care Funds

Health care funds invest heavily in pharmaceuticals and health care organizations—both of which are here to stay. Although the group suffered during the chaos surrounding the efforts to introduce health care legislation, how can you go wrong in the long run with stocks like Pfizer, Johnson & Johnson, Bristol-Myers, Squibb, Abbott Laboratories, Merck, Eli Lilly, and U.S. Healthcare?

The Fidelity Select Health Care Fund showed a 21.4% profit in 1994, even when the Dow was under a doctor's care. Fidelity Select Medical Delivery was up 19.8%. Putnam Health Sciences had a 15.2% gain.

Now that health care reform has been transferred to the intensive care unit, the funds in this group are breathing normally again, and their collective pulse is starting to beat rapidly, ready to resume their favorite exercise: climbing.

As the private sector moves to control medical costs, HMOs should continue to enjoy increased demand. The pharmaceutical companies, always innovative, figure to prosper, particularly as the aging population requires more drug products for health maintenance.

Unless health care reform legislation comes back from the

dead, health care funds could be a prescription for a healthy future. They are volatile—small dosage is recommended.

Index Funds

Index funds are designed to duplicate mechanically the performance of a stock average such as the S&P 500. If you think the stock market will go up in the long run, invest in an index fund—you will have purchased a little bit of everything.

Index funds come in all flavors, but most of them are vanilla. If the stocks in the index you purchased go up, you win; if they go down, you lose. You don't have to worry about the ability of the portfolio manager. Like the Maytag repairman, he has practically nothing to do.

Index funds buy all the stocks, or a representative sample of all the stocks, on a given index. The most popular index is the S&P 500, but you can buy funds that mimic the S&P 400, the S&P 100, even the Wilshire 5000.

The S&P 500 index is market-weighted, meaning that the bigger companies in it get a larger share of your investment. The S&P 400 index slices off the top 100 of the biggest corporations, leaving smaller companies, many in the emerging growth class. The S&P 100 index retains only the largest of the 500 companies.

There are even variations on those themes. The Dean Witter Value-Added Equity Fund divides its portfolio evenly among all 500 stocks on the S&P 500 Index. The IDS Blue Chip Advantage Fund is computer-driven—it analyzes all the stock on the S&P 500 and buys only the highest-rated ones in each industry. Vanguard's Small Capitalization Stock Fund tracks the Russel 2000 index; the Vanguard Extended Market Fund duplicates the Wilshire 5000. You can buy a precious metals index, a gold index, a gas index, an international index, even the Domini social index, which is composed of "socially conscious" stocks.

Indexing the bond market is more difficult because of constantly changing maturities, but the Vanguard Bond Market index tries to match the Salomon Brothers Broad Investment Grade bond index.

You may have wondered why there is no Dow Jones index fund. The reason is that Dow Jones has refused to allow its distinguished name to be used for such a purpose.

There are a lot of advantages to owning index funds. They have the lowest costs of all funds because there is no need to pay high salaries to portfolio managers or exorbitant fees to investment advisers. Because they are always fully invested in a predetermined group of stocks, there is little portfolio turnover and not much in the way of transaction costs.

Mostly, however, buying index funds is like kissing your sister.

International Funds

Montgomery has an Emerging Markets Fund. Lexington has a Worldwide Emerging Markets Fund. Oppenheimer has a Global Emerging Markets Fund. Janus has a Worldwide Fund. Founder's and G.T. Global both have Worldwide Growth Funds.

How do you tell the players without a program? What are the differences between these funds?

Morningstar has divided all international funds into four groups: Europe stock funds; foreign stock funds; Pacific stock funds; and world stock funds. All in all, in early 1995, there were more than 100 international mutual funds.

The first classification is easy: Europe stock funds invest in companies located in Europe. Foreign stock funds invest in companies located in Europe, Japan, Latin America, and the Pacific Rim. World stock funds invest in all of the above, plus the United States. Pacific stock funds invest in Japan, Hong Kong, Malaysia, Singapore, and Australia.

How are they doing?

Europe Stock Funds

Funds that invest in European stocks have a very mediocre record. Five years ago there were only 10 European stock funds, and together, said Morningstar, they had a "strikingly unexciting record."

As of this writing, Europe is reportedly starting to come out of its recession. This, along with the benefits (to them) of the weakened American dollar, has resulted in some modest recent gains.

None of the funds in the Europe group has earned a Morningstar 5-star rating. In fact, there is only one 4-star-rated fund among them—the Dean Witter European Growth Fund, which had a 1994 profit of 6.9%.

Foreign Stock Funds

Foreign stock funds, which invest all over the world except the United States, have very few common characteristics. Some put their money in long-established, giant corporations like Nestle, Ciba, and Bayer, while others shake the dice with small, supposedly growing companies in Latin America and the Pacific Rim. Some of them have done very well; some of them have done very badly; some of them have done a little of both.

Foreign funds which were heavily invested in Latin America (and most of them were) had heavy losses when Mexico devalued the peso in 1994. Fidelity's Latin America Fund finished 1994 with a loss of 23.2%. On the other hand, Fidelity's Emerging Markets Funds had a profit of 81.7% in 1993.

Investing in foreign funds is like the roller coaster ride you enjoyed as a youngster. Lots of excitement and a little scary.

Pacific Funds

The recent history of Pacific funds is not very encouraging. The group lost a lot of money in 1994 due largely to major declines in the Hong Kong and Malaysian stock markets.

Even the four Pacific funds that earned Morningstar's 5-star ratings did not have star years.

The Dean Witter Pacific Growth Fund lost 17.6%. Morgan Stanley Asian Equity had a 15.8% decline. The T. Rowe Price

New Asia Fund dropped 19.2%. The Putnam Pacific Growth
Fund almost made it with a loss of only 0.5%.

The Pacific region certainly has long-term growth prospects, along with unusually high risks due to political and economic volatility. Caution is recommended.

World Stock Funds

It is impossible to find any commonality among world stock
funds they invest in many different countries and in many different industries in those countries.

The G.T. Global Growth & Income Fund put 57% of its
money in Europe and nothing in Japan. Merrill Lynch's global
holdings funds had only 15% in Europe and 31% in Japan. The
Paine Webber Atlas Growth Fund had nothing in Japan and 26%
in the United States.

The result is that these funds swing back and forth as the
economies in their favorite countries prosper or decline. Leader-
ship in this group keeps changing—the fund that topped the
charts one year is at or near the bottom the next year.

The two funds with the best three-year records are Janus
Worldwide and Prudential Global Genesis. But hold on—the
funds with the best five-year records are neither of these; they
are Keystone American Global Opportunity and Templeton
Growth.

Big gains are possible for the venturesome investor, but
extra care is required in making a prudent selection.

International Funds Overview

This is a very risky area where there are many unknowns. If you
can handle the risk and figure the unknown, you can enjoy some
stunning results.

There are two principal reasons to invest in international
funds:

1. Many foreign economies are growing faster than ours.
2. The profitability of an international fund is not dependent upon the progress of any one country's economy.

If the United States stock market suffers a major setback, just about every domestic fund will be seriously affected. If the German stock market falls, losses—theoretically—will be softened by gains in Japan or Latin America or in other parts of the world where an international fund might be invested.

There is yet another factor which has proved to be an enormous profit maker for international funds but which could become a serious drain on their performance: currency exchange rates.

A Diller a Dollar

Strong foreign currencies mean strong performances by international funds. Strong foreign currencies and a weakened U.S. dollar can mean humongous profits for international funds. Said *Barron's:*

> The dollar has been the most important factor affecting returns on the more than $70 billion of international funds.

From 1985 until 1987, the U.S. dollar lost nearly half of its value in the foreign exchange market. In 1985 the Fidelity Overseas Fund had a phenomenal profit of 78.6% and the Paine Webber Atlas Global Growth Fund earned 65.6%.

In the period from 1988 to 1992, the U.S. dollar was relatively flat against most foreign currencies. International funds, as a group, went up 63% during that period, but U.S. equity funds gained 85%. In 1993 the U.S. dollar was under attack, and Fidelity's Emerging Markets Fund had a 81.7% advance; the average international fund gained 40.2%.

1994 was an exceptional year in which exceptional outside forces influenced the performance of international funds even more than the condition of the dollar. The Mexican peso devaluation severely damaged many international funds. The sudden increase in U.S. interest rates was followed by rate increases in some European countries, weakening the funds invested there. The international funds that prospered—and some did—achieved their gains thanks to wise stock selections and the accelerating economies of some emerging countries. In fact, 1994 was the only year since 1987 when the condition of the dollar in relation to foreign currencies was not the overriding factor in determining the results for most international funds.

It will not be ever thus.

Potential international fund investors should understand that a 20% drop in the value of a foreign currency relative to the U.S. dollar is the same as if there had been a 20% drop in that country's stock market.

Of course, it works the other way around, too. But the major point is that even if you own the most substantial, fastest-growing stocks in a given country, if the currency of that country performs badly in relationship to the U.S. dollar, you probably will lose a lot of money.

The U.S. dollar is very weak now. Are you willing to place a large bet that it will never regain its strength?

Absent the currency problem, some international funds will continue to produce handsome results from a careful selection of foreign stocks and, frankly, from being invested in the right country at the right time. But if the dollar regains its power and foreign currencies weaken, you had better learn the international phrase for "Outta here."

Yes and No

As I stated earlier, one of the reasons to invest in international funds is that the economies of many foreign countries are growing faster than we are. Two-thirds of the world's biggest and best companies are located outside the United States, including all 10 of the world's largest banks and seven out of 10 of the largest automotive, insurance, and financial companies. The United

States has had the top performing stock market only once since 1976.

International funds, as a group, have had a great overall performance record. According to Ibbotson Association, Inc.:

International stocks perform better than domestic stocks two-thirds of the time.

And *Worth* magazine reported that:

Academics and others have shown that, over time, portfolios with a proper mix of overseas investments invariably outperform those with no foreign exposure.

International funds have certainly proved to be popular with investors. In 1993 international funds produced an average return of plus 43%, and the inflow of new money reached record proportions. In January 1994 $18 billion was put into mutual funds; $10 billion of that, or 55%, went into funds invested in foreign stocks.

There are, however, some serious disadvantages:

1. You have no way to make sober judgments about the stocks your fund is buying. When a domestic fund selects General Electric or Coca Cola, you understand exactly what it owns. What do you know about a Korean telephone company or the Eurobonds of the Republic of Argentina? Did you ever hear of Mannesmann? The AIM International Fund owns more than $5 million of its stock.

2. In truth, what do you know about the economies of Australia, Taiwan, Brazil, or Spain? Did you know, for example, that the stock markets of 12 countries have plunged more than 50% or more? The stock markets of Greece and New Zealand lost more than 70% of their value between 1990 and 1995.

3. In most foreign countries, there are simply not that many substantial companies for your international fund to purchase.

Portfolio managers have had to buy second- and third-class companies. And, while many domestic portfolio managers are concerned about risk, most international portfolio managers are addicted to risk.

International funds may be the wave of the future. You could also wave good-bye to your money. On balance, however, the evidence seems to indicate that some international funds should be included for any investor with a sense of adventure.

Natural Resources Funds

"Natural Resources" funds invest in oil, gas, mining, basic commodities, and precious metals.
That's true—sometimes.
The T. Rowe Price New Era Fund is described as:

Investing in companies that own or develop natural resources.

Its largest single investment is in Wal-Mart!
One of the reasons some funds in this group depart from their original mission is that natural resources have not been so "resourceful." As a group, these funds have failed to beat the S&P 500 in 10 out of the last 12 years. They have been buffeted by world forces that affect the price of oil; by the weather, which influences the price of gas; and by the alarming fact that portfolio managers, in a frantic effort to increase return, have gambled on commodities, one of the riskiest of all investments.

Precious Metals Funds

Gold is one of the safest investments you can make.
Gold is one of the most volatile, dangerous investments you can make.

Every portfolio should have at least a small percentage of precious metals funds as a hedge against inflation.

The ownership of precious metals funds should be limited to Mississippi river gamblers and fanciers of Russian roulette.

There is validity in all of those statements, but some are more true than others.

Precious metals funds, as a group, have produced some enormous gains. Their losses, surprisingly, have not been all that catastrophic by comparison.

Over the past 12 years, the biggest gain of this group occurred in 1993 when the average total return was 84.8%. In 1986 and 1987, this category averaged profits of 34% and 36%, respectively. The biggest losses were minus 26.8% in 1984 and minus 17.7% in 1988. For an investment that has a reputation for being perilous, that record is not half as frightening as generally supposed.

The volatility of precious metals funds depends upon where they invest their money. The Benham Gold Equities Index Fund and the Fidelity Select American Gold Fund cannot, by charter, invest in South African gold stocks. These funds tend to be less erratic, with lower highs and higher lows.

The Lexington Strategic Investment Fund, on the other hand, is 100% invested in South African gold stocks. In 1993, it had a fantastic return of 267%. In 1992, it lost 60.7%.

Most other precious metals funds have varying balances of both North American and South African gold stocks. They usually end up in the middle, with few spectacular gains and few stupendous losses.

Conservative investors—even more moderate ones—seem to shy away from precious metals funds in an automatic knee-jerk reaction that these funds are too dangerous for the average pocketbook. In view of their records, which are not as terrifying as their reputation, a modest investment in precious metals funds could prove to be very profitable, particularly if inflation suddenly bursts out all over.

Small Company Funds

Funds that invest in small companies have shown large profits.

This, after all, is the essence of the American way of life. Get an idea, find a niche, work your rear end off, and tomorrow Warren Buffett will be asking you for advice.

Every big company started small. Our future rests, not on the aging smokestack industries of yesterday, but upon the feisty, upstart smaller companies that are nimble enough to grasp the golden ring while the giant bureaucratic corporations are looking for paperwork rather than opportunities.

Many small company funds have discovered these emerging companies and cried Eureka! all the way to the bank. Fidelity's Low Priced Stock Fund had a 46.2% profit in 1991, followed by 28.9% and 20.2% in the next two years, and finished 1994 on the plus side. The PBHG Growth Fund hit 51.8% in 1991, 28.5% in 1992, 48.5% in 1993, and completed its successful run with a profit in tough 1994. There are not a lot of fund groups that have shown such consistent gains over the recent years.

You probably would not recognize most of the group's heaviest investments. Intervoice, Wisconsin Central Transport, CUC International, and Atmel are not names that have ever been introduced to either Mr. Dow or Mr. Jones. But small company funds like them, and investors like the results they have produced. The Seligman Frontier Fund, for example, invests in Xilinix, Ceridian, Nu-Kote, and Cynge Designs, but with a bush league lineup like that, Seligman was in the top quintile of its group in both 1993 and 1994.

The Twentieth Century Giftrust Investors Fund fattened on a diet of such nonhousehold names as Ultratech Stepper, Fastenal, Three-Five Systems, and Methanex. Don't laugh: in 1994 when the average equity fund bit the dust, it produced a 13.5% profit.

Here's the future. Long range investors who can handle some volatility will be hard pressed to find more attractive risk/ reward vehicles. Over the years, the stock market has gone up. Over the years, the good little ones become good big ones.

Technology Funds

This is where the action is. Fasten your seat belt, call your cardiologist, and enjoy the thrills (and chills) of flying in the stratosphere.

In the past five years, seven of the top ten performing mutual funds were technology stocks. Fidelity Select Computers had the second-best record of all funds in 1994.

Morningstar lists only seven technology funds—and six of them are from the Fidelity family. Five of these have 5-star ratings, and all are considered to be above average or high in exposure to risk.

Except for the Alliance Technology Fund, which is diversified, all of the other funds in the group concentrate their investments in a special sector of the technology spectrum.

The Fidelity Select Developing Communications Fund focuses on wireless technologies such as cellular and paging equipment and wireless transmission. Fidelity Select Electronics is big in semiconductors—more than 65% of its portfolio is in semiconductor stocks. Fidelity Select Computers is obviously into computer manufacturers and computer hardware suppliers. Fidelity Select Software and Computers, contrary to its name, puts most of its money into networking. Its single largest investment is in Cabletron Systems. The Fidelity Select Technology Fund concentrates on a combination of computers and semiconductors.

Many Wall Street pundits and financial writers have been predicting the death of technology funds. To date, as Mark Twain said, these reports have been premature.

Technology funds can raise your blood pressure—and increase your bank account. They can also make you wish that technological progress had stopped with the invention of the quill pen.

Bond Funds

Bond funds are usually referred to as "fixed income" funds. That is a dangerously inaccurate statement.

Bond funds do not provide any type of fixed income, in any way whatsoever. "Fixed income" refers to the interest paid by the bond issuers to the fund. Period.

It does not mean that you are guaranteed to get a fixed return from the fund. It does not mean that just because there is a steady flow of money into the fund from its investments that it will absolutely make a profit. It does not mean that bond funds, even the most conservative ones, are absolutely safe. They aren't going out of business, but in a time of rising interest rates, many of them are going to lose money.

Yield

Too many bond fund investors chase yield. When yield goes up because of rising interest rates, the value of the fund's shares go down. Yields keep changing: that great yield you get today may look embarrassingly puny six months from now. And some very attractive yields are—seriously—too attractive. Some funds have achieved great yields by taking awesome risks. Pump steroids into a horse and it will probably win its next race. Sooner or later, however, it will break down.

The Fundamental U.S. Government and Strategic Income Fund has been crowing about its high yield for years. The payoff, however, is in total return. At the end of 1994, this fund yielded 10.4%—a very handsome number. Its total return was minus 25.6%.

Volatility

Many bond funds have a reputation for being very stable, with no excessive movements either up or down, particularly when interest rates are not fluctuating wildly. The facts are to the contrary.

Here is the total return record of corporate bond funds over the past six years:

1989:	10.9%
1990:	6.2%

1991:	16.4%
1992:	7.3%
1993:	10.3%
1994:	−3.9%

Those figures look like they are from an equity fund group, not from a staid, quiet, conservative bond fund group.

Interest Rates

If interest rates are rising, bond funds are exactly where you should not be. Since 1994, the Federal Reserve Board has been increasing interest rates in an effort to keep inflation in check. Should inflation persist, Fed chairman Alan Greenspan will persist, and bond funds will take another beating.

The day will come, however, when interest rates flatten or go down. When and if that happens, you can make an absolute fortune in bond funds. The worst bond market of all times was between 1979 and 1981. Long-term Treasuries were yielding 15%, and many investors swore they would never buy a bond fund, ever again.

They made that resolution on the eve of the greatest bull market in bonds that ever existed, before or since.

Types of Bond Funds

Morningstar divides bond funds into several classifications: convertible bonds, high-yield corporate bonds, corporate bonds, high-quality corporate bonds, Government adjustable-rate mortgage bonds, Government Treasury bonds, Government bonds, and municipal bonds.

Convertible Bond Funds

Convertible bonds are simply bonds that can be converted into stock. According to Morningstar, funds dealing in these hybrid securities:

offer the upside potential of stocks, without the violent downdrafts.

Great! Why aren't they in everyone's portfolio?
The reason is quality—or the lack thereof.

Convertibles are a cheap way for corporations to issue debt, and the market has been inundated with low-grade paper. Many of the funds in this group have a majority of their portfolios in below-investment-grade bonds. The one inexorable rule of economics is: the higher the return, the higher the risk.

High-Yield Corporate Bond Funds

These funds are called "high yield" because they invest principally in junk bonds. The yield is high—the risk is often higher, depending upon which fund you buy.

Michael Milken gave junk bonds a bad name. Except for 1990, when 10% of the underlying firms issuing them went into bankruptcy, their record as a group has been very gratifying for adventurous investors.

In 1991 the group produced a return of plus 36.8%, followed by an increase of 16.6% in 1992 and a profit of 18.9% in 1993. While they, too, were adversely affected by rising interest rates in 1994, their losses were less than those of most other bond funds. They ended the year off only 3.8%.

Morningstar has given its 5-star rating to eight high-yield corporate bond funds—some indication that there is substance and stability in an area often considered too hazardous for most investors. In fact, many of these funds—the Main Stay High Yield Corporate Bond Fund, the Merrill Lynch Corporate High Income Fund, and the MFS High Income Fund—are actually rated as low-risk investments.

Clearly, these funds are not for neophytes. You cannot get high yields without considerable risk, despite what Morningstar says. If the economy prospers, the chance of widespread defaults are reduced and the high yields are very attractive. But you will be flying high, and you had better be prepared to bail out at the first sign of a recession.

Corporate Bond Funds

The term "corporate bond" covers a wide and sometimes wild variety of investment strategies. It does not mean that these funds put their money into the quality bonds of major corporations. Many of these funds focus on the lowest grades of corporate paper, in foreign bonds or in longer-maturity U.S. government instruments. Some are involved in sophisticated and complex techniques which scare the average investor (or should). The Strong Short-Term Bond Fund, for example, deals in inverse floaters, Z-tranches, and principal-only and interest-only strips.

Do not invest in anything you don't understand.

Corporate bond funds are particularly sensitive to interest rate increases and, like their junk bond cousins, can be severely damaged by the questionable quality of their below-investment-grade holdings.

Corporate bond funds are only for the knowledgeable investor who is comfortable with the exotic—and sometimes chaotic—nature of the various investment strategies employed.

High-Quality Corporate Bond Funds

These are the funds that do invest in the obligations of America's most substantial corporations, such as Coca Cola, Exxon, and General Electric. Some of them maintain high quality standards by putting most of their assets into U.S. Treasury bonds and other government-backed instruments.

While these investments sound gilt-edged, they are not without risk. Rising interest rates take their toll on even the best corporate issues and on all grades of governmental securities. Most high-quality corporate bond funds lost money in 1994. It is true that, as a group, high-quality corporate bond funds had the best 1994 overall corporate bond performance—but only because it lost the least.

In a climate of rising interest rates, these funds are subject to two different drags on their profitability. They carry lower-coupon issues which do not help to offset any capital losses. And, because of the liquidity of their high-grade paper, their prices rapidly reflect all interest rate-induced fluctuations.

Whither interest rates? Whither inflation? Unless you are sure you know the answers, the term "high quality" will not help you much.

Government Adjustable-Rate Mortgage Bond Funds

These funds traffic in adjustable-rate mortgages and mortgage-related securities backed by the U.S. government and in some private mortgage-related securities.

A typical portfolio might be made up of instruments issued by the Government National Mortgage Association (Ginnie Mae), the Federal National Mortgage Association (Fannie Mae), the Federal Home Loan Corporation, and private paper issued by such companies as Citibank and Sears.

It is a byzantine world. In order to understand it—and invest in it—you must be familiar with such terms as CMO floaters, I/O inverse floaters, Cofi Arms, Libor, and the CMT Index. It is a bizarre bazaar, suitable for habitation only by mortgage bankers and very experienced professionals.

Government Bond Funds

Guaranteed?

Yes, the instruments held by these funds are guaranteed against default by the full faith and credit of the United States government.

Guaranteed return?

No.

In 1994 this category suffered more than any other taxable fixed income group. Its epitaph might read: Here lie government bond funds, murdered in cold blood by the Federal Reserve Board.

In 1994 investors rushed to the exits like there was no to-morrow—and there may not be. The group's assets were re-duced by almost 20% by the end of the year.

Government bond funds mean high risk when interest rates are soaring. If you had invested $100,000 in Fidelity's Spartan Long-Term Government Bond Fund at the beginning of 1994, you would have lost $14,300 by October.

You mean investors in government bond funds can actually lose their money?

To be sure.

And, to be sure of a proper return on your investment, you might want to wait until interest rates stabilize. In the mean-while, have you checked the rates on certificates of deposit lately?

Government Treasury Bond Funds

What is the difference between government bond funds and government Treasury bond funds?

Government bond funds invest in Ginnie Maes, Fannie Maes, and some but not many Treasury securities. Government Treasury bond funds invest almost exclusively in United States Treasury bills, notes, bonds, and zero coupons, with very minor holdings in non-Treasury paper.

Sounds wonderful. Safe like you were home in bed.

Safe, they are; wonderful, they are not.

Here again, dat ole debbil, the Federal Reserve Board, is the major influence upon results. Funds with longer maturities were seriously damaged in 1994. Even those that managed to shorten their maturities were barely able to escape the general debacle.

If you want the safety and security of government Treasury issues, buy them yourself. You can pick the maturities and yield that suits you, and you won't have to worry if Alan Greenspan has caught a cold.

Speaking of interest rates, did you ever wonder what actually happens when the Federal Reserve Board raises interest rates? Chairman Greenspan does not pick up the telephone to call all the banks in America and tell them, "Hey, fellows, guess what? Interest rates are now up a half a percent."

The Federal Open Market Committee, which is the Fed's policy-making arm, instructs the New York Federal Reserve Bank to sell government securities in the open market. That reduces the supply of reserves in the banking system and increases the Federal funds rate—the rate banks pay when they borrow from each other.

When (and if) the Federal Reserve decides to reduce interest rates, it just reverses this procedure. The New York Federal Reserve bank buys government securities and pumps money into the banking system, lowering the Federal funds rate.

While I am on the subject, permit me to ask you some very sneaky questions about the Federal Reserve System.

What is the Federal Reserve System?

A branch of the United States government?

No.

A United States government agency?

No.

An agency created by Congress and reporting only to the President of the United States?

No.

The Federal Reserve is a private organization owned by a group of banks.

It is, in reality, a privately owned banking cartel. A federal court specifically ruled that the Federal Reserve System is a private banking monopoly. It is owned by more than 300 bank shareholders who were classified by a proviso in the 1913 Federal Reserve Act as Class A shareholders.

Municipal Bond Funds

Yes and no.

First, the no.

How would you like to own some municipal bond funds

holding bonds issued by the city of Newark or Detroit or Los Angeles or, in fact, almost any of our larger cities? Many of these cities are flirting with bankruptcy. Most of them are finding it extremely difficult to raise taxes in order to meet budget demands. And the unintelligible bookkeeping procedures of many major cities would cause most accountants to take up needlepoint.

Wait a minute. Most of the municipal bonds issued by these large cities and other municipalities are rated by Standard & Poor's and Moody's. What's the problem?

The problem is that these ratings are mostly meaningless.

Do these rating services complete a hands-on examination of the municipality's books?

No.

Do these rating services employ outside accounting firms to go over the books and issue a report?

No.

Well, what do they do?

They accept the figures supplied by the municipality and issue a rating on the basis of whatever they were told. The municipality can supply any information it likes—there is no one checking the accuracy of the "facts" presented.

Which is exactly what happened with the Orange County, California, disaster.

Right up to the day of bankruptcy, Standard & Poor's rated the county's general obligations as AA, and Moody's gave them an AA1 ranking—both indicating high degrees of safety.

You don't believe that these rating services simply accept as gospel what they are told? Here is what each of them had to say:

Dan Heimowitz, Moody's director of public finance, said, "We were told that the derivative position was smaller and that it was hedged."

John Reichert, head of surveillance for Standard & Poor's, said, "Our analysts relied upon the county's assurances that there was plenty of cash to cover losses."

"We were told." "We relied." Incredible. There is convincing evidence that both Standard & Poor's and Moody's still believe in the tooth fairy.

Now, just calm down here. Certainly, municipal bond fund portfolio managers are smart enough to stay away from questionable issues.

If they are all that smart, how come, as a group, their second-largest holding is in the bonds issued by the Denver airport? Collectively, they own more than $200 million worth of these securities.

Now, they can lose their money—and their luggage.

After all that, how can there be a Yes?

Investors love the tax-free status of these funds. Shareholders rack up all those returns without having to pay anything to the government.

For investors in high tax brackets, good municipal bond funds provide a reasonable margin of safety, high yield, and not a nickel for Uncle Sam.

Closed-End Funds

Would you believe that in this dog-eat-dog (bear-eat-bull?) world, you can buy a dollar's worth of assets for ninety cents?

Cross my heart and hope to buy—it's true.

Closed-end mutual funds.

Open-end mutual funds and closed-end mutual funds are hissing cousins. First, the similarities.

They both consist of portfolios of stocks, are professionally managed, and have the same objectives—to make money for their shareholders in the form of dividends and capital gains. All of their portfolios can be analyzed the same way. And there are closed-end domestic and international funds, single-country funds, and bond funds—just like open-end funds.

End of similarities.

Open-end funds issue an unlimited number of shares, and you can always redeem your holdings by selling them back to the fund at their net asset value. Closed-end funds issue a limited number of shares—and that's it. These shares trade on the stock exchange and are bought and sold just like stocks. In order to sell your closed-end fund shares, a broker acting on your behalf must find a buyer who may pay a little more or a little less than the last quoted price of your fund. You cannot buy existing closed-end shares from the fund—you must use a broker to bid in the open market.

Perhaps the most significant difference between the two types of fund is that the share prices of closed-end funds are determined by market forces—the actions of buyers and sellers—and not by the value of the fund's holdings.

Sometimes, the share price of a closed-end fund will exceed its net asset value—which is the sum of all the stocks it owns. That is because there are more buyers than sellers—the buyers believe that the fund's share price represents a good value and is due to go up. When that occurs, the fund is said to be selling at a premium—you must pay more per share than the value of each share if, hypothetically, all of the fund's assets were sold. At one point, the Bergstrum Capital Closed-end Fund was selling at a 25% premium—the price of its shares was 25% more than the total of all of the stocks in its portfolio.

In the early 1990s, most closed-end funds sold at a discount—meaning that the price of their shares was less than the combined net asset value. At the end of 1994, the average closed-end fund was selling at about a 10% discount.

Well, now, how about if we rush in and pick up a few of these bargains? How wrong can it be to buy a publicly traded stock that is selling at 10%, even 15%, below its real value?

Very wrong.

Late in 1994, for example, the Worldwide Value Closed-end Fund was selling at a 19.6% discount. Reason? Its net asset value had gained just 0.01% a year for the preceding five years. Investors were convinced that the fund wasn't going anyplace and a cheap price for shares was no substitute for poor future prospects.

Catherine Gillis, editor of the *Morningstar Closed-end Fund*

Report, said, "If you buy a mediocre fund with a great discount and it stays mediocre, you're stuck."

Closed-end funds usually involve greater risk than open-end funds. Even if you buy at a steep discount, it is quite possible that the discount could get even bigger. In falling markets, closed-end funds often wear a double hex sign: the value of the portfolio drops and the discount widens.

Many closed-end funds use leverage to increase returns, borrowing against assets in order to buy more and more stocks. When the market declines, or when interest rates spike up, closed-end funds usually take a bigger hit than open-end funds.

At the end of 1993, a group of 92 closed-end regional and country funds traded at an average premium of 12%. International fever was sweeping the marketplace, and everybody wanted to invest in foreign markets. In early 1995 these same closed-end funds were trading at an average discount of 15%.

When a closed-end fund swings from a 10% premium to a 10% discount, the investor loses 18% of his capital. If the net asset value drops at the same time, losses can reach 30%, even 40%, rather quickly.

Closed-end mutual funds offer some advantages. On the other hand, would you buy a bargain parachute?

Six

Mutual Fund Newsletters

Can You Read Them and Reap?

"With pen and pencil, we are learning to say nothing more cleverly, every day.

—William Allingham

In this chapter, in alphabetical order, are reviews of 25 mutual fund newsletters.

Cabot's Mutual Fund Navigator

If you used this newsletter to navigate the mutual fund seas in 1994, you are either sinking or you have sunk.

In January 1994, its "Fund of the Month" recommendation was the Robertson-Stephens Contrarian Fund. It wrote, "This fund will be topping the performance charts a year from now."

Well, just about a year from then, the Robertson Stephens Contrarian Fund showed a total return of minus 4.82%, underperforming the S&P 500 by a whopping 8.4%.

Yes, I know it is not completely fair to judge a fund by just one year's performance. But this fund started in 1993, so there is no long-term record to consider. It ended 1993 with a net asset value of $11.41; a year later that was down to $10.53 after a distribution of 25 cents a share in dividends.

Sure, if you live long-enough, the Robertson Stephens Contrarian Fund may eventually prove to be a winner. But when a newsletter selects it as the "Fund of the Month" and says, "This fund is a great buy now," you don't really expect that it would immediately start going in the wrong direction and continue heading that way.

In February 1994 the *Cabot Navigator* selected the Mathers Fund as its new "Fund of the Month." This fund seeks capital appreciation.

It hasn't found it yet.

At the end of the year, Mathers was off 3.44%—not horrendous in a difficult market, but not a 5-star-quality performance after its all-star buildup. In early 1995 *Kiplinger's* magazine listed it as a fund that has gone steadily downhill.

In February 1994 the *Navigator* started touting gold funds, with the statement "Long term, the trend is with you."

It kept plugging gold funds month after month for nine months. Then, suddenly, on the back page of its December 1994 issue, it said, "In the gold fund group, all funds are rated sell."

If you are going to pay for predictions, it seems reasonable to expect your newsletter to get some of them right.

Ringold Rating: Forget it.

$86 a year. (508) 745-5532

Fidelity Focus

This newsletter, published by the Fidelity family of funds, is issued free to all Fidelity fund investors.

No pain, no gain.

It is, truly, a house organ. It promotes—guess what?—Fidelity funds. It never suggests that you might want to sell any

Fidelity funds. If any Fidelity funds have a miserable year—and some do—you will never learn about them in *Fidelity Focus*. Indeed, you won't learn very much that you don't already know. *Fidelity Focus* is just a slick, four-color corporate brochure.

But, why not? It's free. And better (slightly) than reading a cereal box.

Ringold Rating: You can't knock Santa Claus.

Fidelity Insight

In order to attract new subscribers to this newsletter, its publisher, Eric Kobren, sends out a promotional piece titled "Fidelity Profit Alert." In it, he claims that his model portfolios, made up of only Fidelity funds, beat the S&P 500 by several zillion dollars over a seven-year period. He does, indeed, have an excellent previous record.

But three of his four model portfolios lost money in 1994. That is not very impressive for someone who calls himself "the Master of Mutual Funds." A considerable number of Fidelity funds showed excellent 1994 profits, but Kobren did not have them.

Fidelity Computers was up 20.5%. Medical Delivery delivered a 19.8% gain. Electronics was up 17.2%, Japan plus 16.5%, to name just a few. None of these winners was in any of his portfolios.

On the other hand, he did have Canada, down 12%; Balanced, down 5.3%; Small Cap, down 3.3%; International Growth & Income, down 2.9%; and Precious Metals, down 1.1%. His four model portfolios ended the year with 10 different funds, half of which were losers.

He is also guilty, in his January 1995 issue, of being both highly selective and very deceptive.

In a column titled "And The Winner Is," he writes:

> In a field of Fidelity's 37 diversified equity funds, which one had the highest return for 1994? You already know the answer: Blue Chip Growth.

The reason for this paragraph and its unabashed self-praise was that he had been plugging the Blue Chip Growth Fund for sometime and was now trying to get readers to believe that he had picked the overall winner.

But, notice please, his arbitrary inclusion of the word "diversified" in his description of Fidelity's equity funds. That, by his too careful and capricious definition, eliminated a large number of Fidelity funds that had performed considerably better than the Blue Chip Growth Fund.

The real winner was Fidelity's Health Care Fund, up 21.5%. Second was Computers, and third was Medical Delivery.

Kobren had none of them. The objection is not that he didn't have all the winners—who does?—but that he deliberately misinterpreted the facts to make readers believe that he did.

Kobren's long-range record is, indeed, exemplary. But one wonders if his future results will not be squeezed and fudged and reinterpreted to show that he is all he says he is: a "Master of Mutual Funds"—or a master at making readers believe he is a master.

Ringold Rating: Okay, if you have enough grains of salt.

$177 a year. (617) 369-2500

Fidelity Monitor

Like *Fidelity Focus* and *Fidelity Insight*, this newsletter follows Fidelity funds only. It is "independent," which means that it goes wrong all by itself.

It maintains five different model portfolios: income, growth and income, growth, international, and what it calls its select system.

All five portfolios were losers in 1994.

The income portfolio—its most conservative model— consisting of two Fidelity bond funds and the Fidelity Asset Manager Income Fund, was down 2.1% at year's end.

The growth and income model was off 3.7%. The growth portfolio was down 2.1%.

The international fund portfolio had a sizable loss—minus 15.0% in a year when a number of international funds showed very respectable gains.

The "select system" model lost 0.9%.

Five out of five. That is batting exactly 0.000%.

In its January 1994 issue, *Fidelity Monitor* listed some of the Fidelity funds that had very profitable records for 1993: Precious Metals, up 111.6%; American Gold, up 78.7%; Brokerage, up 49.3%; Leisure, up 39.6%.

Fidelity Monitor had none of these.

There was a disturbing note in its February 1994 issue which didn't do very much to instill confidence in this newsletter. It said:

> After introducing our International Model and Growth & Income Models, our original matrix has become a bit outdated. On reviewing the matrix in our December issue, some subscribers remarked that they still weren't certain about which models to follow. Others found the calculations too complex, and a few remarked that they would have to hold up to 10 funds for their particular mix. This month there is a new matrix.

Subscribers should not have to pay for on-the-job training.

Beside the model portfolios, the *Monitor* carries very little that is new or particularly useful.

Ringold Rating: Not remotely worth the money.

$96 a year. (800) 317-3094

5-Star Investor

The *5-Star Investor*, published by Morningstar, is a calm, quiet—even understated—voice of reason in a newsletter world that is often shrill, shallow, and overheated.

No hype, no hot tips or financial mumbo-jumbo

That's the way *5-Star* describes itself, adding:

Instead, we provide unparalleled data and commentary designed to make you better informed investors.

You can believe every word of it.

5-Star gives readers sound, authoritative, long-range advice, simple explanations of complex subjects, common-sense investment strategies, and just enough statistical background to make mutual fund investing easily understandable.

Most issues have 40 pages, half of which are devoted to a simple-to-follow statistical track record of 500 of the most popular and promising funds. The other half consists of readable (strange word in the hyperventilated world of mutual fund reporting) articles that will help you understand what is going on and show you how to profit from it.

A sampling of article titles indicates its unique approach and down-to-earth viewpoint:

"When and Why Funds Beat the Market"
"Savor the Flavor of Single-Country Funds"
"Forging an Investment Plan Between Hope and Reality"
"Do Too Many Captains Sink the Mutual Fund Ship?"
"New Asset Allocation Strategies"

Many issues carry "The Last Word" columns by John Rekenthaler, the astute editor of *Morningstar Mutual Fund Reports,* or by Don Phillips, the publisher, who is easily the most knowledgeable voice in the mutual fund industry. Their contributions alone are worth the price of admission.

Ringold Rating: 5 stars. The very best.
$79 a year. (800) 876-5005

Fund Exchange

Paul Merriman is a one-man supermarket for mutual fund investors.

He publishes the *Fund Exchange* newsletter. He is the portfolio manager of five Merriman funds. He has written two books on mutual funds, is a featured speaker at financial seminars, and has made guest appearances on PBS's *Wall Street Week* and the *Nightly Business Report*. He also plays the lead in a two-hour video called "How To Succeed In Mutual Funds." In addition, he offers a variety of private management services for individual investors and pension plans.

Merriman is a market timer. Between April 1994 and early spring 1995, his Merriman Switch model portfolio was almost 100% in money market funds. His bond portfolio was 100% in money market funds for nine of the 12 months of 1994. His gold switch model was in money market funds for half of 1994 and 100% invested for the other half. Only his international switch fund was fully invested all year, except for one month.

The bewildering problem, however, is that his newsletter does not report how he did when he was fully invested. The gold fund, for example, was 100% in the market in January 1994, 100% out of the market for four consecutive months, then back in again for four consecutive months, then out again. Nowhere, in any of his newsletter issues, is there any information on how this timing strategy actually worked.

His international model was fully invested for 11 months. There is not the slightest mention, anywhere, of its performance record.

Merriman has 11 other model portfolios. While the individual funds within them are specified, the only other information he provides about them is their telephone numbers.

Weird.

One can only come to the conclusion that he has something—or a lot—to hide. Every other newsletter with model portfolios prints its records every month, win, lose, or draw.

Merriman also devotes a lot of space in his issues to making the case for market timing over a buy-and-hold strategy. But there is absolutely no factual evidence that his methods are any more profitable. Market timing has its exponents—what it doesn't have, in this case, is any evidence to support the claims he makes for it.

In one issue, he compared four funds in a buy-and-hold mode versus a market timing technique. Guess what? Market timing produced the best results. Big deal. If I had my choice of any four funds out of more than 6,000 to compare against any one strategy, I could make the result come out any way I wanted by selecting only the funds which proved my point. A false comparison is not admissible evidence.

Merriman is all show and no go.

Ringold Rating: How do you define "huckster"?

$125 a year. (206) 285-8877

Funds Net Insight

For many years, Eric Kobren published the *Fidelity Insight* newsletter, which limited its coverage to funds from the Fidelity family. In August 1994, he unveiled *Funds Net Insight,* which comments on all funds, including Fidelity's.

It is difficult to understand how an individual who has spent most of his professional life involved with Fidelity (he was once a Fidelity portfolio manager) can suddenly become an expert in the thousands of non-Fidelity funds. Either he focused his attention and research on Fidelity, which is more than probable, or he shortchanged his subscribers by dividing his efforts, which is hard to believe.

Now, he is trying to compete with newsletter publishers who have spent their entire business lives, not as specialists in one family of funds, but as generalists who have always covered the entire mutual fund industry. Kobren brings nothing new to the party.

His new newsletter is—another newsletter. It contains the same news that you will find in other publications. It contains the same thumbnail sketches of various funds that are analysed with more authority by other newsletters. And it has the same four page of pure fund numbers which are available almost everywhere else.

Each fund is given a Buy, Sell, or Hold rating. These recommendations may prove useful for Fidelity funds, but it is highly questionable if Kobren is that knowledgeable about all the other funds that were never under his scrutiny before. If Dan Sullivan or Sheldon Jacobs offer a recommendation, a reader can presume some background and rationale to the advice. It is not enough just to put the words "Buy," "Sell," or "Hold" alongside mutual fund names.

At this writing, his portfolios are only six months old— much too soon to make any judgments. But it is not too soon to observe that what the mutual fund world doesn't need is just another newsletter.

> Ringold Rating: A terrible waste of newsprint. All those trees chopped down for no good reason.

$177 a year. (617) 235-2477

Fund Profit Alert

If you have the stomach—and the checkbook—to be a constant trader, in and out, in and out, in and out, then you might profit from the *Fund Profit Alert* newsletter. But you had better get an open phone line because you are going to spend half of your life buying and selling, selling and buying, buying and selling. And you will need to hire six certified public accountants to keep track of your transactions.

The September 1994 issue of *Fund Profit Alert* said:

> In the All-Fidelity Sector Fund Portfolio, we reduced our exposure in Fidelity Japan from a 25% allocation to a 12$1/2$% allocation. Also, we recommended purchasing a 12$1/2$% allocation in Fidelity Select Paper and Forest. In the All-Fidelity Global Portfolio, we reduced our exposure in Fidelity Japan from a 25% allocation to a

12¹/₂% allocation. In the No-Load Sector Portfolio, we sold the 12¹/₂% allocation in T. Rowe Price International Japan.

The October 1994 issue states:

In the All-Fidelity Global Portfolio, we sold our 12¹/₂% allocation in Fidelity Japan and purchased a 25% allocation in Fidelity Fifty. In the All Fidelity Sector portfolio, we sold the remaining 12¹/₂% allocation in Fidelity Japan and purchased a 25% allocation in Fidelity Select Biotechnology. In the No-Load Global Portfolio, we sold our 25% allocation in Invesco Pacific Basin and purchased a 25% allocation in Invesco Health Sciences.

In just a few months with this newsletter, you will run out of your free exchange privileges and go broke paying redemption fees. You will also have to give up your daytime job. (On the other hand, you can drive the I.R.S. crazy just trying to report your cost basis on all these transactions.)

Ringold Rating: I sold my 25% allocation in Insanity and purchased a 9¹/₈ allocation in You've Got to Be Kidding.

$200 a year. (800) 327-8833

Graphic Fund Forecaster

Fred Hohn, the publisher of the *Graphic Fund Forecaster*, is a market timer and technician. If you speak Greek fluently, you might be able to make sense out of his newsletter.

Example: he uses what he calls the Stochastic Oscillator and says:

We use a 5-day exponential on the %K and %D lines to smooth and delay crossing signals. Both the RSI and stochastics use a 0–100 scale which is the computational result range.

He also uses a series of charts to determine when the market is going to go down. He writes:

Charts used in determining the Down Index summary value include: DJIA, NYSE, Hi-Lo channels, DJIA Stochastic Oscillator, S&P 500 Stochastic Oscillator, Odd Lot Daily Balance Ratio, the Titanic Syndrome, A/D NYSE Comparison "Opposite Steps," Empirical Trend Forecast, NYSE Declining Quantity, NYSE Advance-Decline Strength and RSI Charts for the Sample Portfolio.

So why didn't he use some of those fancy charts to help stem some of the losses? Three of his five sample portfolios produced minus figures for 1994. His Invesco Strategic Fund was off 11.5%; his Select Fund 2 was down 9.26% and the Select 1 portfolio was minus 1.98%.

The Growth International 1 Fund was up 4.28%, and Growth International 2 managed a gain of 0.91%. It hardly seems worth all that effort.

Nine of the 12 pages in this newsletter are given over to charts of the funds followed. On each chart, there is a line representing what is called the Relative Strength Index. Says the publisher:

If the RSI value is high (80–100), you know that sooner or later, the fund will turn down. If the RSI value is low (10–30), sooner or later, the fund will turn up.

Sooner or later??? You could go broke waiting for sooner to become later and vice versa. Sooner or later, every fund goes up or goes down.

One more example: He writes:

What to do? Clearly, an indicator is needed to provide discrimination. Our solution is a verification indicator which works most of the time.

Most of the time??? How would you like to have a doctor who is right most of the time?

If you are an M.I.T. graduate, with honors; a professional statistician with good eyesight to follow all those wavy lines; and a mathematician who not only understands Einstein's theory of relativity but can explain it, then, maybe—maybe—this newsletter is for you.

But I doubt it.

Ringold Rating: #&^%!(&*^$ + @>\# minus.

$145 a year. (508) 470-3511

IBC/Donoghue Bond Fund Advisor

This newsletter is of interest only to fixed income investors, and it is not as comprehensive or as useful as the *Income Fund Outlook Newsletter*, described just below.

It does not cover as many bond funds. It does not offer buy-sell-or-hold recommendations. It does not estimate future returns. Its statistical data are purely historic and provide nothing of value that is not available in more detail in its rival publication.

The only continuous feature that is different are the three model portfolios it runs. Unfortunately, all of them were in the minus column for 1994. Through 1994, the Total Return model portfolio consisted of only one fund—the T. Rowe Price High Yield fund. However, the newsletter admitted that it had picked a bummer and, by the time you read this, it will have been replaced "by a similar fund, either from Vanguard or Fidelity." Subscribers could not have been exactly overjoyed when this "Fund Of The Year" was one of the worst performing fixed income funds of 1994.

While confession may be good for the soul, it is not great for the pocketbook. In its last 1994 issue, the newsletter wrote:

> We continue to hold the junk bonds since our buy recommendation in April 1991. The downturn this year has been the worst since the buy recommendation, but we remain optimistic that the performance of these funds will improve.

In the immortal words of Samuel Goldwyn, "Include me out."

> Ringold Rating: Fixed income investors: skip this one and take a look at the Income Fund Outlook.

$95 a year. (800) 343-5413

Income Fund Outlook

This is the Bible for fixed income investors.

Five of its 12 pages provide an extensive statistical history of most of the existing bond mutual funds. This information tells you the fund's primary holdings (e.g., "Ginnie Mae, Gov't. Agency, Corp.AAA"); the average portfolio maturity in years; the risk rating; and the yield.

In addition, there are unique and useful columns titled "Projected Total Returns," covering both one- and five-year periods, with different estimates, depending upon whether future rates go up or down. There are also one- and five-year past performance ratings, as well as loads and fees, if any; and annual expense ratios and minimum investment requirements. And most funds are given a current recommendation rating, from Avoid to Hold to Buy to Best Buy.

There is another page and a half containing the identical information for tax-free bond funds.

Two pages are given over to money market funds. Here the

categories include "Safety Rating," "Yield Forecast," "30-Day Yield," "Minimum Initial Investment," and "Total Assets."

The gem of this section is found in the "Editor's Analysis," which contains succinct statements that sum up the benefits or disadvantages of every money market fund listed, including "Poor yield-safety ratio"; "mediocre yield"; "excellent yield-safety record"; and "below average yield."

Another table provides the same information for tax-free money funds.

The back page is a must-read for all short-term, fixed income investors. It lists the best F.D.I.C.-insured banks by name, telephone number, rate offering, and yield of certificates of deposit for seven different maturities, from 30 days to five years. (All rates are based upon a $5,000 minimum deposit.)

There is yet another chart on the front page which gives you an at-a-glance look at the best buys in long-term bond funds.

And if all that isn't worth your money, you also get two pages of current commentary on general economic and market conditions, along with the latest bond fund and money market fund news.

If you are a fixed income investor, you simply have to subscribe to this newsletter. You really have no choice.

Ringold Rating: Is there a mark higher than Excellent? $100 a year. (800) 442-9000

Independent T. Rowe Price Adviser

As its name indicates, this newsletter follows only T. Rowe Price funds.

It started 1994 on the wrong foot and went steadily downward thereafter.

In its January 1994 issue it stated:

Interest rates may climb modestly. Rates are so low now that it isn't hard to imagine them bouncing a bit higher—but I don't expect a big increase.

Six Federal Reserve increases during 1994 might just possibly cause you to lose a wee bit of confidence in this newsletter.

In February 1994 it recommended a T. Rowe Price fund, with the following statement:

The High-Yield Fund will prosper as the economy continues to recover, and it's one of the safest junk bond funds around.

In July, however, it admitted that the:

High-Yield Bond Fund was already down 1.7%.

In the same issue, it made some changes in its model portfolios:

We sold 20% of our investments in each of the funds in our model portfolios. We used the proceeds to add equal amounts of New Era and Japan to each portfolio.

By December, New Era was off 4.3%, and Japan was down 6.2%.

There are three model portfolios. Each one was a loser at the end of 1994. The three portfolios together held 16 T. Rowe Price Funds. Each one of the 16 was in the minus column at year's end.

An unfair short-term criticism?

All three portfolios were started in January 1994. Three, five, 10, 50 years from now, they may turn out to be real winners. But wouldn't you prefer to back an adviser who manages to get off to a good start—especially when a fair number of T. Rowe Price funds turned in highly acceptable performances for the year?

Ringold Rating: The T. Rowe Price Adviser is not worth the price.

$139 a year. (800) 435-3372

Independent Adviser for Vanguard Funds

This newsletter covers only Vanguard funds—and it does it very professionally. If you are a Vanguard fan, buy a front-row seat. It was voted the best financial advisory newsletter by the Newsletter Publishers Foundation for two years running.

Each issue contains a close-up interview with a Vanguard portfolio manager; two pages of charts detailing the long-range performance of every Vanguard fund; a "Best-to-Buy" list; and a "Fund Focus" section which provides an in-depth analysis of a variety of Vanguard funds, each carrying a buy, sell, or hold recommendation.

The newsletter is fiercely independent, taking more than occasional potshots at Vanguard or one of its funds:

> Over the past years, Morgan Growth has gone from bad to worse. Vanguard can't seem to figure out how to make this fund work. Quite frankly, this fund is a mess.

And:

> We ran some tests on Vanguard's risk numbers and found that they underestimated each fund's risk by 11% to 12%.

Nor did it bring everlasting joy to the heart of Vanguard's chairman, John Bogle, when it disclosed his 1993 Vanguard compensation of $3.3 million.

Its three-year model portfolio record was excellent. Conservative Income was up 38.1%; Conservative Growth, up 51.1%; and Aggressive Growth, up 55.1%. And it achieved those results with considerably less risk than exists in the overall stock market.

While its future may rest on whether Vanguard funds rise or fall, this newsletter is very savvy about the mutual fund industry, extremely knowledgeable about the inner workings of

Vanguard funds, and very alert to economic changes that can significantly affect your investments.

> Ringold Rating: If you are invested in a lot of Vanguard funds, make another investment in this newsletter.

$139 a year. (800) 492-6868

Moneyletter

The only thing that is different about the *Moneyletter* is that it publishes 26 issues a year. However, it does not contain enough that is valuable or interesting to warrant those extra issues.

Its advice tends to be bland and cliché-ridden, closer to "a penny saved is a penny earned" than to innovative recommendations backed by solid research or accompanied with an in-depth, searching analysis of the funds in question.

Typical of this sort of nothingness are the profiles it usually runs on its spotlighted funds. Just about every one of these is based upon quotes from the fund's portfolio manager and are really only self-serving advertisements. Portfolio managers are not world-famous for their reluctance to promote their own funds. A public relations release from the fund itself would serve the same purpose.

In a promotion piece sent by William Donoghue, its publisher, you were made an offer that simply cannot be refused. It was a red-hot opportunity to "become a millionaire in your lifetime."

The line forms here. Please do not shove.

The copy reads:

The Easy Way To Make $1,000,000.

$10 a week, at 20% or more per year for 30 years—tax sheltered by your IRA—comes to $1,000,000.

"20% a year or more per year for 30 years." In the whole history of the stock market, it has never gone up 20% a year for

30 years. It has never gone up 20% a year for 15 years. No investment of any kind, anywhere, at any time, has ever gone up 20%
a year for 30 years.

That's ridiculous. That's laughable. That's nonsense.
That's Donoghue.

By the way, his fund picking is not much good, either. This
is what he had to say about his Venturesome Model Portfolio,
which was heavily invested in international funds in 1994:

> It was all bad news on the international front. Our
> Japan funds continued to struggle and Preferred Inter-
> national was hurt badly by the slide in Europe. Also,
> T. Rowe Price New Asia plummeted as concerns over
> another rate hike here gripped the Southeast Asian
> markets.

> Ringold Rating: Somewhere between a D and a D
> minus.
> $127 a year. (508) 881-2800

Mutual Fund Buyer's Guide

This newsletter is practically obsolete.

Twenty-two of its 24 pages contain mutual fund performance figures—information that is readily available to you in
Morningstar, the Value Line Mutual Fund Survey, *The Wall Street
Journal*, and *Investor's Business Daily*, in most big city newspapers, in most financial publications, and on the Internet.

Here, for example, is the information it lists for the Magellan Fund:

> Type of Fund (growth); Type of Investments (diversi-
> fied stocks); Safety Rating (7.5); Ranking in Up (A) and
> Down markets (D); Worst Ever Loss (−36% 8/87–12/
> 87); Correlation Vs. S&P 500 (76%); Vs. Bonds (13%);
> Yield (0.9%)

It also provides performance figures for one, three, and six months; one, three, five, and ten years; telephone number; minimum initial investment; sales and redemption loads, if any; annual expense ratio; max tax load; portfolio turnover percentage; next capital distribution; total assets.

Some of that information is important; all of that information is available elsewhere.

If you are a numbers freak who gets a big kick out of reading page after page after page of nothing but figures, and if you don't like Morningstar, newspapers, and financial publications—and you don't belong to a library—well, then, maybe. Otherwise, this non-newsletter newsletter is of little value.

Ringold Rating: Nothing but numbers makes me numb.

$80 a year. (800) 442-9000

Mutual Fund Forecaster

This is one of the very few newsletters that attempts to predict one-year profit performances.

Here are some of the predictions it made in its January 1994 issue—and the final results:

Fund	Prediction	Result
ABT Emerging Growth Fund	+11%	−9%
Acorn	+10%	−5%
Aim Constellation Growth	+10%	+1%
American Captalization Emerging Growth	+10%	−7%
Berger 100	+ 9%	−7%
Brandywine	+11%	Even
CGM Capital Development	+12%	−23%
Fidelity Contrafund	+10%	−1%
Fidelity Equity Income I	+ 9%	Even
Invesco Dynamics	+10%	−2%
Kaufmann	+11%	+9%
MSF Emerging Growth	+12%	+4%

Oakmark	+ 10%	+ 7.5%
Oberweis Emerging Growth	+ 11%	− 3.5%
PBHG Growth	+ 12%	+ 5%
Putnam New Opportunity	+ 12%	+ 3.5%
20th Century Giftrust	+ 9%	+ 11%
20th Century Ultra	+ 12%	− 3.5%

Out of 18 predictions, it guessed right once. Half of the funds it predicted would gain 9% or more lost money.

There is nothing left to say. Except good-bye.

Ringold Rating: Good-bye.

$100 a year. (800) 442-9000

Mutual Fund Investing

Jay Schabacker, publisher of this newsletter, has been called the "unquestioned king of the mutual fund advisory business." While he is no longer the only one at the top, he certainly deserves his royal robes.

Formerly a rocket scientist who worked on the Titan space program, Schabacker has over a 19-year period produced results which, indeed, rocketed into outer space. The sum of $10,000 invested when he launched his newsletter would have been worth more than $125,000 in 1995. Over the 18-month period from mid-1993 until the end of 1994, his "Best Buys" enjoyed a 30% return. No other mutual fund newsletter came even close.

He has been right on target with most of his predictions. In January 1994 he wrote, "Don't expect much from the U.S. stock market this year."

In the same issue he said:

As interest rates rise, capital losses in long-term bond funds will eat into yield, leaving bond investors with new losses.

There were not a lot of newsletter publishers who called that turn so early on.

In March he wrote:

Steer clear of retail, health care, broadcast and media, and consumer product sector funds. These funds took quite a beating during the recent market downturn. And I expect their performance to remain lackluster throughout the rest of the year.

Pretty accurate—and you do get the idea that Schabacker is not afraid to take a stand and make his position known in simple English sentences.

In March he plugged hard for the T. Rowe Price New Era fund. It ended the year up 5.3% in a year when other funds in its group suffered serious setbacks.

Schabacker runs three model portfolios: Growth with Income; Growth; and Maximum Growth.

Over the past two years when the S&P showed a 7.43% gain, his Growth with Income model was up 15.36%; Growth was up 18.87%; Maximum Growth, up 22.59%. For 1994 all three portfolios showed a profit—nothing sensational, but then again, most model portfolios lost money.

Over the longer term, his model portfolios and recommendations have an outstanding record. In mid-1994, the *Forbes* columnist Mark Hulbert wrote:

While assuming just 33% of the risk, however, Schabacker has achieved 70% of the market's return. Now that's worth betting on.

In his last 1994 issue, Schabacker, out on his usual limb, said that in 1995 the Dow could go to 5,000.

He also wrote:

For a stake in the most explosive growth opportunity around, buy Montgomery Emerging Markets or Fidelity Emerging Markets. Investing in emerging markets is the single best way I know to grow your money between now and the year 2000.

This book went to press in summer 1995. So how did he do?
Ringold Rating: One of the best.
$187 a year. (301) 424-3700

Mutual Fund Strategy

The writer and editor of *Mutual Fund Strategy* is Bert Dohmen. This is the third time he has tried to sell a mutual fund newsletter.

His first publication was called *Worry-Free Investing*. It crashed after the 1987 crash when, among other terrible things, his portfolios were margined to the hilt.

His second effort, in 1992, was called the *Mutual Fund Profit Strategy Letter*. In the promotional efforts for this one, he made just a few unbelievable claims, such as:

Forget 20% or 30%. I'm talking big profits.
500%! 600%! More!

There is really no sense in going any further after reading that paragraph. But his current ravings are, well, amusing. In the March 1994 issue he wrote:

By late this year potential criminal charges may become a possibility against the current occupants of the White House.

Dohmen edits his newsletter from Hawaii. How do you say "get lost" in Hawaiian?
Ringold Rating: Don't be ridiculous.
$175 a year. (800) 777-5005

Mutual Fund Strategist

The story behind the *Mutual Fund Strategist* is more interesting than the newsletter itself.

For 23 years, Charles Hooper was a chief master sergeant in the U.S. Air Force. After returning to Vermont from Germany, he took a job in the post office sorting mail because 250 of his job-seeking resumes had resulted in no interviews.

While in the Air Force. Hooper invested in mutual funds—in increments of $25. He slowly developed a primitive timing model based mostly on a book by the now discredited charlatan Nicholas Darvas (*How I Made $2 Million in the Stock Market*). When Hooper's index rose 10% from its low, he bought mutual funds; when it fell 10% from its high, he sold.

This strategy—after some significant refinements which Hooper did not make—is called "momentum investing," and it works—sometimes. It claims, like the Dow theory, that stock market trends persist for a long time. You should get in when the upward trend is under way and out after its climb has clearly ended. You won't buy at the bottom or sell at the top, but you can catch most of the big trends.

In the early 1980s the trending market was in his favor, and his profits were enormous. So, in 1992, he sat down at his dining room table and typed the first issue of the *Mutual Fund Strategist*. He sent it to newspapers and financial publications, hoping for some publicity. Nothing. He took a classified ad in the then *Changing Times* magazine and received—three subscriptions.

Then, Mark Hulbert began tracking the newsletter for the Hulbert Financial Digest. The rising markets in the mid-1980s, before Black Monday in 1987, made Hooper look like a genie and a genius. In 1985 Hulbert ranked the *Mutual Fund Strategist* first out of eight mutual fund newsletters.

Subscriptions started pouring in, and, in 1986, Hooper quit the post office. These days, he has around 6,000 subscribers and he also manages close to $100 million worth of investors' money; investors pay him 2% a year to buy and sell mutual funds on their behalf.

So how has he been doing recently?

Not so well.

He has three model portfolios. For 1994, his Agressive Portfolio was minus 23.6%. His Sector portfolio and his Diversified Growth portfolios both just managed to eke out very marginal profits.

Forbes magazine said:

> In recent years, Hooper has not kept up with the market.

The *Mutual Fund Strategist* is a typical example of newsletters that look great when the market is flying high, but whose results disintegrate when the air gets choppy and some turbulence sets in.

Hooper has a system that once worked. Damn near anything worked when the marked jumped up like Michael Jordan.

Nobody knows how the stock market will fare in the remainder of this century, but the general consensus seems to be that it will go through some difficult weather. If that proves to be true, Hooper's "system" may go down in flames.

Ringold Rating: Don't fly the unfriendly skies with
Hooper.
$149 a year. (802) 658-3513

Mutual Fund Timer

Dan Sullivan, the publisher of *Mutual Fund Timer,* believes that investors should either be 100% invested in mutual funds or 100% out of the market, parking their at-risk capital in money market accounts until it is time to go back into equities again.

And he puts his own money where his mouth is.

In August 1988 he invested $100,000 of his own funds on behalf of his *Mutual Fund Timer* newsletter. Since then, he has been in and out of the market many times. Exactly six years later, by August 1994, he had produced a profit of 125.2%, which works out to 15.10% a year on an annualized basis. His profit picture was not affected through the remainder of 1994 because he got out of the market entirely in early spring of that year. His money market interest produced more profits than most active funds.

If you follow Sullivan, you will miss some profit opportunities because he usually tends to get out of the market early, but you will avoid most of the downturns and take fewer losses than if you were a buy-and-hold investor. Over the indicated six-year period, he has been fully invested 73% of the time and in money market funds 27% of the time.

Is there a great reward at the end of the market timing rainbow? Is there a payoff for getting off the train and sometimes not getting back on again soon enough?

For the 10-year period beginning in 1980, the compound return of the S&P 500 was 17.6%. A $10,000 investment would have grown to $50,591. If, however, you had been out of the market during its worst times, that $10,000 would have grown to $231,225—almost six times the profits of a buy-and-hold believer.

In the market downdraft that lasted only three months (from July 16, 1990, to October 11, 1990), here is what happened to some of the country's best-known funds:

Twentieth Century Growth	− 27.5%
Twentieth Century Ultra	− 28.2%
Scudder Development	− 30.4%
Kaufmann	− 31.3%
Stein Roe Capital Opportunity	− 39.0%
Oberweis Emerging Growth	− 39.0%

During that period, Sullivan was out of equities and into money market funds. As a result, he actually showed a profit of $2,648.

The trick, of course, is to be able to predict when the signal light is going to turn red and when it is ready to flash green again. Sullivan has constructed a series of indices which has enabled him to make those predictions with uncanny accuracy.

Mark Hulbert, the *Forbes* columnist who has tracked hundreds of market newsletters over many years, says:

> The *Mutual Fund Timer* is one of the few services that beat the market over three and a half years through mid-1992, gaining 87.6% compared to 60.3% for the Wilshire 5000. In addition, this newsletter's gain was turned in with less risk than the market as a whole, so on a risk-adjusted basis, it beat the market by an even greater amount.

To be a market timer, you have to have the emotional capacity to get out of the market, even if it is still going up. And you have to have the restraint to stay out when it blips upward in what is known as a bear trap. On both the upside and the downside you will miss some profits, but if you have faith in the fellow calling the signals, you will also avoid serious losses. Sullivan preaches that it is better to give up the profits than try to make up the losses.

History is on his side.

Ringold Rating: If you embrace the concept of market
timing, there is no better newsletter.
$100 a year. (310) 596-2385

Mutual Fund Watch

If you like charts, you will love the *Mutual Fund Watch* newsletter.

Each issue is filled with more than 100 charts that are called "high performance" mutual funds. The charts show where the funds have been over the past two years, and the accompanying text attempts to predict one-year and five-year profits.

Mutual Fund Watch is published by the Institute for Econometric Research—the same organization which publishes the

Mutual Fund Forecaster, reviewed earlier in this chapter. Evidently, the editors of these two sister publications do not talk to each other, even though they are housed in the same building and have access to the same research and statistical information.

As noted above, the January 1994 issue of the *Forecaster* made 18 predictions, 17 of which were wrong. The January 1994 issue of *Fund Watch* predicted the profitability of 14 of the same funds. In every case, *Fund Watch* predicted even higher profits, and its guesses were even worse.

That's terrible—but there is more bad news.

Fund Watch made an additional 23 predictions which were not duplicated. Out of these, it was right—once. All of its examples were projected to earn 10% or more in 1994; 18 of them actually lost money. (Those 23 funds were not handpicked out of the 100 charts. These calculations cover all the funds that the *Mutual Fund Watch* newsletter predicted would earn 10% or more in 1994.)

> Ringold Rating: I tried very hard, but I cannot think of even one reason why you should subscribe.

$100 a year. (800) 442-9000

No-Load Fund Analyst

At $195 a year, the *No-Load Fund Analyst* is one of the most expensive mutual fund newsletters.

It's worth it—if you are a serious, long-range investor willing to devote considerable time and effort to its comprehensive coverage of every aspect of mutual fund investing. Reading its average 40-page issues is like taking an advanced college course with a very interesting professor who is clear, concise, sensible, and very learned.

Every lecture starts out with an in-depth discourse on a subject that is pertinent to your advancement as a student striving to attain better marks for your investments. Topics include:

"Big-Cap Growth vs. Big-Cap Value"
"Derivatives—Damnation or Deliverance?"
"Equity Investing in Emerging Markets"
"Small Company Stocks—Is the Potential Still There?"
"New Funds and Closed-end Alternatives"

Each issue also reviews up to a dozen mutual funds. No statistical charts, no "Best Buy of the Month," no numbers-oriented past-performance comparisons. Instead, you get a thoughtful examination of each fund's investment philosophy, a detailed analysis of each portfolio manager's style, and an objective commentary on each fund's future prospects.

These are "hands-on" inquiries, not reprints of the funds' public relations releases. An editor of the *No-Load Fund Analyst* actually talks to every one of the portfolio managers involved, asks searching questions, and demands straightforward answers—somewhat of a rarity among many portfolio peacocks.

The newsletter runs four model portfolios, all of which began in 1990. Here is their five-year record:

Conservative Income Global Balanced	Up 57.6%
Conservative Global Balanced	Up 58.0%
Aggressive Global Balanced	Up 65.1%
Global Equity	Up 65.5%

These records were all achieved without the no-brainer gains of the roaring eighties.

Please understand: if you are looking for a casual, predigested source of mutual fund advice, this newsletter is not for you. But if you are willing to be a serious student, do your homework, and apply yourself to its principles, you can graduate with high honors—and high profits.

Ringold Rating: One of the very best.
$195 a year. (510) 254-9017

No-Load Fund Investor

Sheldon Jacobs, the publisher of the *No-Load Fund Investor* has a great, even sensational long-term record.

If you had invested $10,000 in his "Best Buys" recommendations when they began in 1982, you would have $71,776—a not too shabby return, particularly when the time period includes the 507-point drop in the Dow on Black Monday 1987.

Jacobs has a great eye for picking new and little-known mutual funds. Way back in July 1986, when the newsletter was only a few months old, he recommended the Gabelli Asset Fund. The fund now has a 5-star Morningstar rating; Morningstar has commented:

> This fund shows investors that they don't have to put up with inordinate risk to find good returns."

In July 1993 *The New York Times* gave 50,000 hypothetical retirement dollars to five investment advisors and proposed that each of them select the appropriate funds that would produce the best results consistent with the conservative nature of the objective.

The *Times's* latest report on this competition was published on April 9, 1995. Sheldon Jacobs was the top performer, with a cumulative increase of plus 21.1%.

Jacobs was one of the first in the industry to point out the many advantages of no-load funds over load funds. And he is one of those pioneers who continues to find gold. If you won't panic if the Dow Jones becomes the Down Jones, then his ability to find new or little-known funds should pan out for you.

Ringold Rating: Better than most.

$105 a year. (914) 693-7420

No-Load Fund X

If you go to Las Vegas or Atlantic City with a lot of money and announce that you have a system to beat the casinos, they will give you free room and board, a front-row seat to their shows, 12-year-old Scotch, and other options of your choice.

The *No-Load Fund X* newsletter has such a system for investing in mutual funds. Please follow the bouncing ball:

First, it takes the average of one-, three-, six-, and 12-month returns for all mutual funds. Then this figure is divided by four, because four different time periods have been used. Then one point is arbitrarily added to each of the top 15 funds in each performance period.

Funds are divided into four groups: "Most Speculative Growth Funds"; "Speculative Growth Funds"; "Best Long-Term Record"; and "Total Return Funds."

An integral part of this system is that you must "upgrade" in order to take the greatest advantage of this process. "Upgrading" is defined as:

Staying in top-ranking funds by progressively selling losers and buying winners.

The five top-ranking funds in each of the four groups is printed in each issue.

There is a slight problem.

In the August 1994 issue, the five top funds in the "Most Speculative" group were Scudder Latin America, Invesco Pacific Basin, Nomura Pacific Basin, Invesco European, and Scudder Pacific Opportunity. By January 1995 not one of these funds was any longer considered the best of its class. Sell all five. Buy five new ones.

In that same August issue, six funds received top rankings. By January 1995 five of them had disappeared. Sell five funds. Buy five new ones.

Similarly with the funds listed as "Best Long-Term Funds." Six were indicated to have the best long-term record to date. By January, all six had been removed and replaced with five new listings. Sell six, buy five new ones.

Same for the Total Return funds. Five were named in August; an entirely new five were picked in January. Sell five more; buy five new funds.

You are now a world-class trader and, I am sure, about to

have yourself committed to the nearest insane asylum. I shudder even to think about your redemption charges.

The newsletter itself admits that, yes, there is this slight problem. It said:

> Brokerage commissions of no-load funds can be a problem, particularly if you are trading relatively small amounts. If you are an aggressive trader, you will soon run out of freebies.

Or out of patience with this nonsense.
Ringold Rating: How about a 1?
$119 a year. (800) 323-1510.

Vantage Point

In a subtitle on its cover, this newsletter calls itself "An Independent Report for Vanguard Investors." Clearly, it is attempting to compete with—and must be compared to—the *Independent Report for Vanguard Investors*. Please don't be confused. *Vantage Point* has very little to offer. It is not very noteworthy, not very interesting, not very useful.

It spent a lot of time and space in 1994 on interest rates and inflation, but its comments were mostly empty generalities available in most popular magazines. It also devoted many issues to looking backward to tell you where you had been. Again, this material is available in most financial publications and in many large newspapers—in more depth and with more practical insight.

It runs five model portfolios. For 1994, two lost money, two showed small gains, and one broke even. Not terrible, but many Vanguard funds did pretty well in 1994 and you would expect a Vanguard specialist to have many, if not most, of them.

The biggest problem with this newsletter is that it has a competitor.

Ringold Rating: Vantage Point provides no advantage.

$129 a year. Vantage Point does not provide its telephone number in any of its issues. The address is: 2927 West Liberty Avenue, Pittsburgh, PA 15216.

The Ringold Ratings Revisited

If you want to subscribe to just one newsletter, the far-and-away best selection is the *5-Star Investor* by Morningstar. It, indeed, rates five stars.

A very close second is the *No-Load Fund Analyst*—provided that you are willing to spend a lot of time with its comprehensive coverage. Serious, dedicated, analytical readers will find that it is well worth its high price.

Seven

The Stock Market and You

"Wall Street is bordered on the West by Trinity Church, on the East by the East River, by frenzy on the North and hysteria on the South."

—John G. Fuller

To prosper with mutual funds, you must have some understanding of the stock market. That's what mutual funds do—they buy and sell stocks and bonds.

If the stock market goes up over a reasonable period of time, most mutual funds make money. If the stock market goes down over a reasonable period of time, you can have a portfolio of the best, 100% gilt-edged mutual funds—you are going to lose money.

It would help, therefore, if you could figure out what makes the stock market go up and down.

Nobody knows.

The unemployment rates drops and more people are earning more money. That's good news—but the stock market goes down.

The dollar weakens and the trade deficit widens. That's bad news—and the stock market goes up. Other times, when the

133

dollar weakens and the trade deficit widens, the stock market goes down.

On January 19, 1995, the Dow suffered a severe decline. *The Philadelphia Inquirer* reported the story with this headline:

Dow Drops 46.77 Points on Rate Fears

The lead paragraph of the article said:

Renewed fears of higher interest rates yesterday pushed stock market prices sharply lower.

The New York Times, on the same day, had an entirely different reason for the slide. Its headline read:

Stocks, Following the Dollar, Fall on U.S. Trade Outlook

Its opening paragraph said:

The stock market followed the dollar, which tumbled in international currency markets yesterday, as the Government reported that the United States economy was headed toward the biggest annual trade deficit in seven years.

No mention of the falling dollar and the trade deficit in the first report; no reference to rising interest rates in the second article.

Claudia Goldin, a Harvard economist, said, "Explanations for why the stock market went up and down belong on the funny pages."

Here are some headlines that appeared late in 1990:

Uncertainty Reigns for U.S. Economy (*The Wall Street Journal*)

The Consumer Has Seen the Future and Gotten Depressed (*Business Week*)

Housing Recession Now Engulfs Entire Nation (*The New York Times*)

Can Your Bank Stay Afloat? (*U.S. News & World Report*)

A few months later, the Dow went up 25%; 1991 was the best year for the stock market in two decades.

Experts?

The experts can't even agree on the condition of the overall economy, which is the basis for most stock market trends.

In February 1995 the Dow passed the magical 4000 mark for the first time. The reason given by most Wall Street professionals was that the Federal Reserve Board had signaled that it was not going to raise interest rates again because its crystal-ball gazers had decided that the economy was slowing down.

But other Wall Street professionals said that the economy was not slowing down. *Barron's* wrote:

The thrust of manufacturing, the peppy tone of cars, rising capital spending, straining capacity both here and abroad and, most of all, jobs and confidence—none of this squares with Mr. Greenspan's or Wall Street's vision of a faltering economy.

A headline in *The Wall Street Journal* on March 6, 1995, read:

Economy Shows More Evidence of a Slowdown

On the same day, a *Business Week* headline said:

The Economy May Be Hotter than Wall Street Thinks

The experts don't agree on what makes the stock market move; they don't agree on the condition of the economy; and they are not very good at picking stocks.

The Wall Street Journal appointed five "investment professionals" to select one stock that he or she thought would make the biggest gains between July 12, 1994, and the end of the year.

Edward Smith, president of a money management firm, picked Amresco as his stock of the year. It dropped 69.9%.

William J. Brady, of Presidio Management, selected the Maxim Group for the one stock to own if you could only own one. It lost 11.4%.

Richard Schmidt, of Stellar Management, opted for Chico's. It went down 58.3%.

When the contest started, the editors of *The Wall Street Journal* picked four stocks by throwing darts at the New York Stock Exchange list.

The darts selections went up 5.3%.

Most so-called experts are reluctant to admit the error of their ways. Not John Hartwell, portfolio manager of the Hartwell Leverage Fund. After the fund's NAV declined 21.4%, he said:

> I failed to anticipate how seriously energy and technology stocks were going to get mauled. I should have been taken out and shot.

That solution is probably a mite too drastic, but what is a poor investor to do—particularly if he does not want to stay poor?

Do it yourself!

Don't pay attention to stockbrokers. They are professional optimists. Would you buy their mutual funds if they told you that the stock market was going to go down?

Don't pay any attention to economists—they predicted seven out of the last six recessions.

Peter Lynch, who was responsible for the success of the Magellan Fund, is neither a stockbroker nor an economist. He is simply one of the wisest men on Wall Street, and he has the record to prove it. He said:

> Your investor's edge is not something you get from Wall Street experts. It's something you already have. You can beat the experts.

Do it yourself!

You should begin by tracking a few very simple economic yardsticks.

There is absolutely no reason for you to get involved with price/earnings ratios, price/book evaluations, advance/decline line variations, and other esoteric symbols dear to the cold hearts of Wall Street pontificaters. Just pay attention to two important measurements: One tracks interest rates and inflation, and the other provides a clear picture of the health of the overall economy. They are the CRB Index and the Index of Leading Indicators. Both appear in most major newspapers.

The stock market likes low interest rates and a low rate of inflation. It gets positively catatonic if interest rates shoot up and rampaging inflation follows.

The stock market did not have a great 1994. A big part of the reason was the continuous increase in interest rates. But the principal reason it did not suffer a major reversal was that the rate of inflation was reasonably under control.

If interest rates start climbing again and if inflation gets out of hand, sell your mutual funds. Put your money into Treasury bills or certificates of deposit. The market does not go up as fast as it goes down. There have been no days in the entire history of the stock market when the Dow has risen 507 points in one day, but it fell that much on Black Monday in October 1987. Sit quietly and wait for the storm to pass.

How do you know in advance whether you should prepare to abandon ship?

The CRB Index, which is issued monthly, is a basket of the prices of 21 basic commodities. Together, they reflect major changes in the rate of inflation. The 21 components of the CRB Index are:

Unleaded gasoline	Gold	Silver
Platinum	Copper	Heating oil
Live cattle	Coffee	Hogs
Soybeans	Sugar	Soybean meal
Soybean oil	Cocoa	Orange juice
Corn	Wheat	Cotton
Crude oil	Lumber	Pork bellies

The CRB Index, over many years, has led all other inflation indexes in signaling major changes in the rate of inflation. If the CRB Index keeps going up, a significant stock market advance is unlikely because it would be predicting an increase in interest rates and the onset of inflation. If it keeps spiking upward, and if each increase is bigger than the preceding one, you will soon hear a loud noise on Wall Street as the stock market comes tumbling down.

The second index you should follow is the Index of Leading Indicators, issued monthly by the government and also published in most major newspapers and in *The Wall Street Journal*.

The Index of Leading Indicators forecasts the strength and weakness of the overall economy. Are we heading for a recession? Are we heading out of a recession? Are we continuing to be prosperous? It combines most of the basic indications of our economic health into one Index. Its components are:

Unemployment claims	Supplier deliveries
New building permits	Plant and equipment contracts
Money supply	Sensitive material prices
Stock prices	Consumer expectations
Average work week	Vender performance
Durable goods orders, Backlog	

Obviously, if this index heads down, you should start heading out. One or two months of downward movement does not necessarily mean that we are recession-bound. Three back-to-back months in the wrong direction, however, are a strong signal that you should lighten your mutual fund holdings. If there is a fourth month of poor results, you would be well advised to sell all of your holdings, go into money market funds or Treasuries, and wait until conditions start to improve.

If the CRB Index heads up and the Index of Leading Indicators heads down, you know there is trouble ahead. These two indexes are taking the country's pulse with 32 different measurements. If they are moving sharply in different directions, you should ask for directions to the exit.

The Dow Jones Industrial Average

Another thing that you should understand about the stock market is that the Dow Jones Industrial Average is out-of-date. It no longer is a true indication of the broad stock market and therefore no longer serves the purpose for which it was originally intended.

A little history, maestro, please.

Back in 1884, Charles Jones got the bright idea of adding up the prices of 11 big companies (mostly railroads), averaging them, and using the result to track the entire stock market. Over the next 44 years, nine more stocks were added. In 1928, 10 new stocks joined the list, bringing the total to 30.

That was 67 years ago—and the number of stocks in the Dow is still 30. Some changes have been made—some companies have merged, others have gone out of business, and a very few have been replaced because they no longer represent a significant part of the U.S. economy.

Even though an almost endless array of new companies has been listed on the New York Stock Exchange, and even though the face of U.S. industry has drastically changed with the advent of the Age of Information, statisticans still claim that the average of 30 stocks is an accurate indication of the entire stock market. (Did you ever try to argue with a statistician?)

The 30 Dow stocks are:

AT&T	DuPont	Minnesota Mining and Manufacturing
Allied Signal	Eastman Kodak	Morgan, J. P.
Alcoa	Exxon	Philip Morris
American Express	General Electric	Procter & Gamble
Bethlehem Steel	General Motors	Sears
Boeing	Goodyear	Texaco
Caterpillar	IBM	Union Carbide
Chevron	International Paper	United Technologies
Coca Cola	McDonald's	Westinghouse
Disney	Merck	Woolworth

The Dow is important only semantically. It is a kind of shorthand that provides a rough—very rough—indication of the trend of the stock market.

If you really want to know how the stock market is faring, follow the S&P 500. It is a much broader index and more truly represents all the listed stocks.

If one of the Dow's most heavily weighted stocks—IBM—takes a hit because of internal factors that affect only IBM, the entire Dow reading is affected, and you get a false picture of the entire stock market. Morningstar, for one, no longer recognizes the Dow. The performance of all of the funds it covers are compared to the S&P 500.

Do not put your faith in false prophets.

Dollar Cost Averaging

You should be familiar with the stock market technique called dollar cost averaging. It is recommended by many professionals as a prudent way to buy mutual funds.

The Wall Street Journal likes it. It said, "People who invest in stocks regularly get the benefit of dollar cost averaging."

Worth magazine likes it. It said, "Dollar cost averaging can minimize the impact of market volatility."

Dollar cost averaging is simply investing a given amount of money in a stock or mutual fund at regular intervals (every month, every quarter, every six months), no matter what has happened to the price, no matter what has happened to the general stock market, or to the economy as a whole.

Do not dollar cost average.

You are agreeing to invest in a mutual fund without any regard for the real world. Stock markets run in cycles; sooner or later cometh the Bear. If the fund you have selected starts to go down and continues to go down and continues to go down, are you really going to keep sending good money after bad? If you stop somewhere along the way, you now own a lot of shares in which you have a pretty good loss.

You will notice that in the example from the *Mutual Fund Forecaster*, the price of the shares never fell below the amount originally paid for them. If the $10 a share price had fallen to $9, then $8, then $7, you would still be expected to send in your money even though it is quite clear that you have picked a loser. Instead of getting out, you get in deeper. Eventually, you may get even. Eventually.

One of the few eternal truths of mutual fund investing is that diversification is the secret for success. With three, four, or more funds in your portfolio, are you going to dollar cost average each one of them? You'll soon run out of money.

And there is considerable evidence that the whole idea doesn't work in the first place.

Richard Williams and Peter Bacon, of Wright University in Dayton, Ohio, undertook a great deal of research in order to compare lump sum investing with dollar cost averaging. Their study covered a 65-year period, from 1926 until 1991.

The results showed that, two-thirds of the time, lump sum investing significantly outperformed dollar cost averaging.

The National Association of Mutual Fund Investors, commenting upon the results of that study, said:

Since stocks have an upward bias and are rising a majority of the time, dollar cost averagers are likely to make future investments at higher prices than lower prices. As a result, the average cost of future investments tends to be higher than the cost of the initial investment. Most of the time, therefore, the initial lump sum investment is made at a lower price than the average price for all subsequent dollar cost averaging investments.

Mark Stumpp, chief investment officer of Prudential Diversified Strategies, compared the historical performance of lump sum investing with averaging over a 69-year period.

Who is in favor of dollar cost averaging? Mostly stockbrokers and mutual fund promoters who are trying to get you as a permanent customer.

Convincing proof of this can be seen in a brochure published by the Investment Company Institute, the lobbying and public relations arm of the mutual fund industry. The dollar cost averaging strategy it advocates is a disgusting example of its arrogant disregard for the intelligence of the average investor.

The brochure presents a hypothetical case involving a quarterly investment of $300. Shares are initially purchased at $25 each so that the buyer receives 12 shares at the beginning of this exercise in naked greed. Four additional purchases are made at the following share prices: $15, $20, $10, and $5.

The Institute gleefully points out that, after an investment of $1,500, the purchaser owns 137 shares at an average price per share of $10.95.

Despite the fact that the price per share has dropped like a rock, the brochure urges you to keep sending in your money. It says:

You invest $300 quarter after quarter, watching the share price fluctuate and then go down. But in the spirit of dollar cost averaging, you keep plugging along.

The price of your shares has dropped from $25 to $5; your fund has lost 80% of its value, and the brochure states:

You can't chicken out now when you see the market dropping.

The sky has fallen, Chicken Little has run for the hills, and you are expected—encouraged—to keep backing a fund that, after 15 months, hasn't shown a profit and, in fact, has lost 75% of its value in just the preceding six months.

Beware of slicks bearing gifts.

Wall Street—Weak?

A chapter titled "The Stock Market and You" would not be complete without some reference to Louis Rukeyser and the television program *Wall Street Week*. More than 10 million people are reported to watch it every Friday, somehow braving the love affair that the pompous host has with himself.

The celebrity guests on the program usually recommend a series of specific stocks. I have read the results of four different studies of these recommendations, and they all have reached the same conclusion:

The stocks go up before the guests appear on the program.

In all, the record of 896 stock selections were traced over four periods of time. It is much more than a coincidence that in most cases the upward action of the recommended stocks occurred in the week immediately preceding the guest's appearance.

The conclusion is inescapable. The guests, knowing what they were going to recommend, told their clients and their friends what the selections would be. The clients and their friends told their sisters and their cousins and their aunts, resulting in a buying spree that sent the prices up.

The prices went up again on the Monday following the program as the public rushed in to buy.

By Friday of the first week, however, the stocks had lost most of their previous gains. Within two weeks, they were back to where they had been before the guest appeared. In the next six weeks, most of the stocks had fallen significantly relative to the market. Over the next 13 weeks, they suffered further losses.

One of these studies was conducted by Robert A. Pari, then an associate professor at Bentley College. He found that the recommended stocks underperformed the market by $2^1/_2$% in the six months after the program and by 4% in the 12 months following the guest's original appearance.

The best selection of the best Wall Street experts—and most of the stocks in the study ended up with losses. Is it possible that the insiders have screwed the public again? Is it possible that they bought these stocks in advance, watched the public rush in and push up the prices, and then bailed out with their profits, contributing to the eventual losses?

All those who think it is possible, please raise your right hand.

Eight

When Should You Sell?

Buying Is Easy; Selling Is the Hard Part

"You can't go broke taking a profit."

—Bernard Baruch

General rule: sell any fund that keeps you up at night.

If a mutual fund worries you for any reason, that is reason enough to get rid of it. Forget the facts—the fact is that your guts are telling you that something is wrong, somewhere. Is the fund worth giving you an ulcer? Your doctor may say Mylanta, but your common sense should say, Enough already. So you have to eat a loss—that's better than having to eat a soft diet for the rest of your life.

You can't make a profit unless you sell. The question is: when?

First of all, how is your fund performing in comparison to the general stock market?

The S&P 500 is up 10% and your fund is down 5%. What are you waiting for?

It should be clear to you that the market is moving in one direction and your fund is moving in the other direction. How much do you want to lose before you finally get the message?

145

Marty Zweig, one of the most astute mutual fund portfolio managers, says, "Don't fight the tape."

The tape—meaning the numbers being posted for all stocks on the various exchanges—is saying that there is something basically wrong with your fund. Otherwise, it would be moving up with the rest of the market.

Obviously, the time frame is important here. A couple of bad weeks is not enough reason to jump ship. But don't wait too long. There are few clearer signs of impending disaster than a fund that continues to lose ground while the rest of the market is going up.

Apples With Apples

How does your fund compare to its peers?

If you have a growth fund, how are the other growth funds doing? If you have an international fund, how are the other international funds doing?

Once a week, *The Wall Street Journal* lists the most recent 30-day performance record of all mutual funds. (So do *The New York Times* and other major newspapers.) Once a week, you should make a list.

Which are the 10 funds in your group with the highest increases? Is your fund among them? Is it included after you have made a list for a month? Three months? How long do you want to wait?

If, over a reasonable period of time, there are 10 funds in your group with higher increases, you must accept the fact that you have the tortoise and not the hare. Ten other funds are thriving—the problem, then, is not with the type of fund you own but with the fund itself. You have compared apples with apples, and yours is rotting. Out!

Managers

Did your portfolio manager leave?

This is not necessarily a reason for you to dump your fund. However . . .

Kenneth Oberman ran the Dreyfus Growth Opportunity Fund for five years. During that time, it ranked twenty-sixth out of 416 funds. He left to go to Oppenheimer. The next year, his former fund lost 15.2%.

When Francis Cabour ran the Pioneer Fund, it was usually included on the *Forbes* Honor Roll. He departed to join Fidelity—the Pioneer Fund never again made it to the Honor Roll.

James Marquez was hired to run the then floundering IDS Progressive Fund. Within two years, he improved it to the point where it ranked sixth out of 568 funds. After he left, the IDS Progressive Fund lagged behind the S&P 500 for five years.

Bill Sams was the portfolio manager of the American Capital Pace Fund (then called the American General Pace Fund). He produced an average annual return of some 33%, 12 percentage points better than the average fund in this group. He left to join FPA Paramount. Pace is now in the bottom quintile of its category.

The Alliance Quasar Fund changes managers more often than the New York Yankees. Prior to 1990 the fund had a profitable record under the management team of Paul Jenkel and Frank Burr. After 1990, it went through seven managers in five years—and ranked in the bottom quintile of its group.

Invesco Strategic Energy has had six managers since its inception, three between 1989 and 1993. It has lost money in four of the five years between 1990 and 1994.

When you see the sign "Under New Management," it should be interpreted as "Danger Ahead."

Managers usually leave for one of two reasons: they have done a poor job and are replaced (in which case you shouldn't have stayed with a fund that was doing so badly it had to fire its manager) or they leave for better jobs. And you, now, are in the hands of the second team. You have been given a wake-up call, and you should make a telephone call.

That's right—call the fund and ask to speak to the new manager. It's your money and he's spending it—what are his future plans? Is the fund's investment style going to change? If your fund had been focused on a given market sector (small capitalization stocks, for example), does your manager plan to continue in this area, or is he considering a move into the issues of larger corporations, where he may or may not have had any previous experience?

He undoubtedly will have a lot of reasons for this anticipated change in emphasis, but you should keep in mind what it was that originally attracted you to the fund in the first place. If, for example, you bought the fund because you felt that the real growth would come from investments in smaller companies— and you will think so—then get out and find another fund that likes small capitalization stocks.

If you are reluctant to bother such a busy man, permit me to tell you a personal story.

Evelyn Ringold, who was mentioned in an earlier chapter, owned a very few shares in the Magellan Fund when Peter Lynch was still running it. She called Fidelity for some information and did not like the way she was treated. So she wrote a letter to Mr. Lynch.

He called her!

If Peter Lynch can take the time to respond to a very small investor, your fund manager can damn well take your call.

Targets

Did you set a selling target?

You should plan to sell before you buy.

Going Up

Decide, in advance, what your upside goal is. Don't fall for that old line about letting your profits run. Most funds, like most stocks, do not go straight up forever and are soon replaced by new favorites. There are very few investors who get in at the bottom and out at the top.

But how do you know when to sell? How do you set a reasonable upside target?

Start by looking at the returns you could get in certificates of deposit and short-term Treasury bills. At this writing, one-year CDs are yielding about 7.0%. Obviously, you should not be satisfied with a fund that returns only 7.0%—you can get that much without any risk. Even a few additional percentage points are not enough to warrant taking any chances with your money.

You should be looking for a return double the CD rate—in this case, 14%. (If the CD rate changes significantly, your antici-pated target should also change.)

Let's see how this plan works:

Suppose the fund you have in mind is selling for $30 a share. You invest $10,000 and are looking for an increase of 14%, or $4 a share, by the end of the first year, when the price should be $34. At the end of the second year, the fund should have added another $5 a share to reach the goal of $39 a share.

If the fund is considerably below that price—and if the CD rate has not changed significantly—you ought to get out. You have set a reasonable target, you have waited two years, and the results have not met your expectation. It is time to retire, espe-cially if other funds in the same category have delivered 14% or more.

Let us say that your fund is at $39 and you still own it. It continues to deliver as anticipated; three years later, it is selling for $45 a share, another 14% increase.

In round numbers, you own 333 shares for which you paid $10,000. You can sell those shares now for $14,985, giving you a pretax profit of $4,985.

Don't sell, yet.

The fund has done everything you asked it to do—given you an annual increase of around 14%. (Don't be tempted by other high-flying funds as long as you are getting a reasonable return for your money.)

Now, watch the price of your fund very closely. You have a good profit and you would like it to continue, but the sectors of the market in which your fund may be heavily invested often have a history of rotating in and out of favor. You want to be prepared to take your money and run.

If this fund of yours, which has steadily advanced for three years now, shows signs of faltering, don't wait for it to give back a sizable part of your profits. Suppose that having hit 45, it goes to 46, then 45, then 44, then 43.5. Out. Out. Out. Take your profit and take your place on the sidelines until you figure out what is happening with the stock market and general economic conditions. Was it your fund whose stocks started to go out of favor, or was the stock market flashing red lights all over the place? In either case, that is what money market funds are for. Park your money and wait.

Some people call this process market timing. It isn't really. It is simply protecting your profits.

Going Down

Now, let's look at it the other way—on the downside. You should decide in advance when you will sell if your fund goes down.

It seems to me that a 10% drop is enough to scare anybody. If you agree, it means that when your fund hits $27 a share, you will positively sell it. You have made a mistake, but your first loss is your best loss. If you want to make money with mutual funds, you have to be disciplined. Don't sit around hoping for a miracle—set a downside selling price in advance, and keep your promise.

The Morningstar *5-Star Investor* newsletter says:

> Sell discipline, once set, must also be consistently applied. It is tempting to bend the rules if a fund is enjoying a run of unusually good performances, but as many respected managers have stated in the past, one doesn't lose money by selling too soon.

The Right Size

Has your fund become too big . . . or too small?

Big boats are difficult to turn around, particularly in stormy weather.

Magellan, the world's biggest fund, cannot suddenly sell any considerable portion of its holdings, no matter what is happening in the stock market.

As of this writing, it owns more than $800 million worth of Motorola stock. Any precipitous sale of large amounts of this stock could start a stock market stampede that would make Black Monday look like the night before Christmas. And portfolio manager Jeffrey Vinik knows that—he has repeatedly said that he must act slowly, selling just a little bit at a time. While he is waiting patiently to reduce his holdings, the price may continue to drop, racking up even larger losses. A small fund, on the other hand, can get out of the way before any serious damage is done.

Inflow, Outflow

A sudden flow of large sums of money into a fund is not necessarily a sign of continued health. It may very well be that a lot of investors have found a promising fund, but too much new money can cause very serious problems. (A lot of funds hang out a Closed sign when their asset base jumps up too high, too fast.)

Some funds with a great deal of new money simply run out of quality stocks to buy in the sector of their concentration. There are only so many good small companies for a small company fund. There is only a limited number of good stocks in many emerging countries. There is only a limited number of risks an aggressive growth fund can take before it is tempted to engage in some wild speculations.

Funds with cash overflows are faced with a terrible dilemma. Do they buy second-class issues or put the extra money into cash or its money market-Treasury bill equivalent? Investing in substandard stocks could mean big losses; keeping large amounts of cash on the sidelines could mean missing a rising market.

There is no absolute guideline to help you solve this problem. You have to be alert. Morningstar reports the asset base of

all of the funds it tracks. It issues a new report on asset bases
changes about every three months. If you note a sizable increase,
another telephone call to your fund is in order. What is your
portfolio manager planning to do with all this extra money?

Your need to be alert is heightened if you see that your fund
has a significantly shrinking asset base.

You should be concerned for three reasons. First, the asset
base may be going down because investors, in very large numbers, have redeemed their shares. While the crowd is not always
right, it is prudent to wonder—what do they know that you
don't?

Second, unusually large redemptions often means that a
fund must sell stocks in order to pay the departing shareholders.
It may have to sell in a falling market, taking considerable losses,
or cut down on its holdings in profitable issues, reducing its
future potential. The only course of action for you is to find the
nearest exit.

Finally, a smaller asset base causes expense ratios to go up.
The expenses don't change, but there are fewer investors sharing
in the costs. Like termites, added expenses eat away at profitability.

If your fund's asset base starts to shrink, don't bother to
find out why. Join the crowd and leave at once. Or sooner.

The Old Grey Mare

Have you changed?

Is your financial situation the same today as it was when
you first bought the fund?

You may have purchased that small company fund at the
peak of your earning years, when risk was not a serious problem. But now that you are reaching retirement, risk is a clear
and present danger. Sell, and find some conservative funds for
your golden years.

It works the other way, too. You may have invested originally when you were just starting your climb up the economic

ladder. Accordingly, you purchased funds with moderate risk, or with an emphasis on a flow of dividends. Times have changed. You have prospered, and you have some money you can afford to lose without materially affecting your lifestyle. Live it up! Sell that moderate fund—or, at least, reduce your holdings and look for an international fund or a small company fund or even a technology fund where you can get significant capital appreciation.

It is indeed difficult to say good-bye to a fund that has continuously produced handsome profits for you. One way to reduce the pain is to ask yourself: would you buy that fund now?

Nine

Learn to Read the Prospectus

Mutual Funds Have a Language of Their Own; Unfortunately, It's Not English

"When large sums of money are concerned, it is advisable to trust no one."

—Agatha Christie

There is no cause for alarm.

Reading a prospectus is not really the same as having root canal work.

It is just a question of knowing what to look for and where to find it and understanding what it means.

A prospectus, in the most simple terms, is just a report that tells you the financial condition of a mutual fund. It also contains a lot of other stuff which sometimes needs to be translated from legal hieroglyphics into simple language. Other times, frankly, it is so obtuse that the decipherers of the Rosetta stone

155

would prefer to be bitten by an asp than to try to interpret its unreadable inscriptions.

But we are going to take it nice and easy and, when this chapter is finished, you are going to prefer reading a prospectus to your favorite comic strip.

The first and most important thing you should pay attention to in a prospectus is the section called "Financial Highlights." It looks something like a balance sheet, and mutual funds are required to reproduce it in the first few pages of the prospectus.

Figure 1 presents the financial highlights section from the prospectus of the Yacktman Fund. It was selected because it is a relatively new fund and because its financial highlights are less confusing than most.

Financial highlights, like Hebrew texts, should be read from right to left. Start with the first line in the far right column, where it says:

Net asset value beginning of period

When the Yacktman Fund started, its shares were issued to the public at $10 each. Now look down to where it says:

Net asset value, end of period

The figure shown is $10.39. That means that the fund made a profit of 39 cents a share between July 6, 1992, when it began, and December 31, 1992, the end of the reporting period.

Back near the top, there is a line reading:

Net investment income

Net investment income is money received from dividends on stocks owned by the fund and/or from interest the fund may have received from cash parked in money market funds or from investments in government securities. The Yacktman Fund earned five cents a share from dividends or interest during the indicated period.

Figure 1. Financial highlights, Yacktman Fund.

	Year Ended Dec. 31, 1993	July 6, 1992(1) through Dec. 31, 1992
Net asset value, beginning of period	$ 10.39	$ 10.00
Income from investment operations:		
Net investment income	0.14	0.05
Net realized and unrealized gains (losses) on investments	(0.83)	0.42
Total from investment operations	(0.69)	0.47
Less distributions:		
Dividends from net investment income	(0.14)	(0.05)
Distributions from net realized gains	—	(0.03)
Total distributions	(0.14)	(0.08)
Net asset value, end of period	$ 9.56	$ 10.39
Total Return (2)	– 6.58%	4.72%
Supplemental data and ratios:		
Net assets, end of period (000s)	$143,024	$74,666
Ratio of expenses to average net assets (3)	1.18%	1.18%
Ratio of net income to average net assets (3)	1.61%	1.49%
Portfolio turnover rate	61.14%	30.94%

(1) Commencement of operations
(2) Not annualized for the period July 6, 1992 through December 31, 1992
(3) Annualized

The next line is:

Net realized and unrealized gains (losses) on investments

Net realized gains is the profit actually made on the sale of stock. Net unrealized gains are paper profits—indicating an increase in the price of some of the stock the fund still owns. If the fund bought a stock at, say, $10 a share and the price went up to $15 a share, the books reflect this $5 a share profit, and the fund still owns the stock.

The total gain in this category was 42 cents a share. Add the two gains together, and you get 47 cents a share "Total from investment operations." That was the profit for the indicated period.

The next two lines tell you how much each shareholder received from the fund in 1992.

Yacktman declared a dividend of five cents a share. This figure is always shown in parentheses, which technically means a loss. It is, indeed, a deduction from the fund's value because it was paid out to investors.

The next line shows that the fund paid out three cents a share in capital gains.

Putting those two lines together shows that the fund paid out a total of eight cents a share to investors in its first six months of operations.

It made 47 cents a share and paid out eight cents a share, a difference of 39 cents a share. The net asset value, then, at the end of the period was $10.39. If you had wanted to buy a share of the Yacktman Fund on December 31, 1992, you would have had to pay $10.39 a share.

The next line, "Total Return," is the profit, before the distribution of dividends and capital gains, expressed as a percentage.

You will remember that the fund's gross profit was 47 cents a share—that is, 4.72% of its starting net asset value of $10 a share. This figure appears on the line for total return.

The corresponding footnote at the bottom of the page states that the total return was "not annualized for the period July 6, 1992, through December 31, 1992."

That accounts for the extra two-tenths of a percent shown in the total return, or 4.72%. (Those of us who count on our fingers would have calculated the total return to be 4.70%.)

The next line is:

Net assets, end of period

The value of all the securities owned by this fund, plus any cash, was $74,666,000 at the end of 1992. (This figure will become more significant later on.)

Now we come to:

Ratio of expenses to average net assets

That is the total of all of the fund's operating expenses divided by the average net assets under management, expressed as a percentage.

Ratio of net income to average net assets

is the fund's total net investment income divided by the average net assets under management, expressed as a percentage.

The final line is:

Portfolio turnover rate

That tells you how often the fund bought and sold stocks during the indicated period. The 30.94% figure is extremely modest, reflecting the fact that the fund was in business for only six months and had little reason yet to sell the securities it originally owned.

There is only one more year to go, so stick around for a while.

Now you start all over again at the top of the second column. The net asset value at the beginning of 1993 is obviously the same as it was on the last day of 1992.

The second line shows that the fund earned 14 cents a share in dividend and/or interest income, up considerably from the previous period because its securities now had an extra year in which to earn interest or receive dividends.

The next line spells trouble.

The figure shown is (0.83), meaning a loss of 83 cents a

share. That loss resulted from a combination of two factors: either the fund sold some shares at a loss, or the value of some of the securities it still owns has gone down. It is a combination of real losses and paper losses.

The line "Total from investment operations" shows a loss of 69 cents a share. The fund lost 83 cents a share from its stock holdings, but it earned 14 cent a share from dividends and/or interest. The difference is the final loss of 69 cents a share.

The next figure shows that the fund distributed to shareholders all of the money it received in dividends and/or interest. There was no distribution from net realized gains. Obvious reason: it did not realize any gains. It lost money.

The net asset value at the end of the period reflects this loss. Subtract the 83 cents a share loss from the beginning figure of $10.39, and the result is $9.56.

The total return, expressed in percentages, is minus 6.58%. The applicable figure here is the 69 cents a share loss from investment operations, after the 14 cents a share distribution of interest and dividend income. That 69 cents a share loss represents 6.58% of the opening net asset value.

Looking at the next line, "Net assets, end of period," and comparing it with the corresponding figure for the previous year, you might ask: if the fund showed a loss, why do its net assets show such a big increase? Where did all this money come from?

From you, the investors. It simply means that a lot of people bought a lot of shares in the fund.

Your next question, of course, is why investors would buy shares in a fund that was losing money.

The answer, in this case, lies in the history of Donald Yacktman, the president and portfolio manager. He had a record of extraordinary performance for many years at his previous fund, and investors figured that the market would eventually recognize the long-range value of his stock selections. (Their confidence eventually paid off—the fund was one of the very few that showed a 1994 profit—up 8.8%.)

The changes in the last three lines, compared with the previous period, are not particularly significant. The portfolio turn-over rate did not double—it reflects a full year's operations rather than the six months' operations shown in the first column.

That's all there is to reading the financial highlights section of the prospectus. Just extract the essential information, year by year: Did it make a profit or show a loss? How much did it make from dividends and interest, and how much did it make (or lose) from its stock holdings? Are its expenses generally in line with those of other funds in its category? Have investors rewarded its performance by buying additional shares (increase in net assets), or have investors lost confidence in this fund (decrease in net assets)?

More Highlights

There are two other sections of the prospectus which require your attention. Both of them are always shown in the first few pages of the prospectus.

The first is:

Shareholder Transaction Expenses

In this section, the fund is required to tell you whether or not it charges a front-end load and exactly how much it is; whether it charges a sales load on reinvested dividends; whether there is a deferred sales load; and whether there are redemption and exchange fees.

The second section is called:

Annual Fund Operating Expenses

In this part, the fund tells you what it charges for managing the fund, whether there is a 12b-1 fee, and the total of all other expenses.

Having read earlier chapters in this book, you will, I hope, avoid funds with a front-end load and 12b-1 funds. And you should cast a careful eye on the last line, which indicates the fund's total operating expenses.

Expenses can be a considerable drag on profitability. You should compare a fund's expenses with those other funds in its group. This information is available in the *Morningstar Reports,* which show the expenses for every fund covered as well as the average expenses of other funds in the same category.

You cannot properly compare the expenses of an equity income fund, for example, with the expenses of an international fund. You must compare expenses intragroup.

"Objectives"

In the first few pages of every prospectus is a statement of "Objectives." In this section, the fund—supposedly—explains its goals and its methods for achieving them.

Many of these so-called objectives are meaningless clichés, clever distortions, or outright lies.

Examples:

The prospectus of Pax World Fund states:

The Fund endeavors through its investment objectives to make a contribution to world peace through investments in companies producing life-supportive goods and services.

What a lovely idea. Here is a fund that certainly deserves the support of peace-loving people everywhere.

So why is its largest holding the H. J. Heinz Company? And its third-largest holding is Campbell Soup. (The concept, I assume, is that we will down the enemy's missiles by firing cans of vegetable soup and bottles of catsup.)

Also included in its holdings are $5,950,000 worth of Nike stock, obviously to prevent a "sneak" attack!

It also owns considerable shares of Liz Claiborne, Circuit City, the Limited, Inc., and Wal-Mart.

. . . contribution to world peace . . . life supportive goods and services.

Even the good guys stretch the truth sometimes.

The prospectus of the CGM Fund states:

The fund's objective is reasonable long-term capital appreciation with a prudent approach to protection of capital from undue risk.

Very reassuring. Sounds like it invests in a lot of blue-chip stocks and gilt-edged bonds. Perfect for your aged Aunt Ethel; ideal for building a retirement nest egg.
Absolutely not.
Up to 5% of its assets may be invested in:

Fixed income securities of a quality below investment grade.

That's junk bonds! Hardly a "prudent approach to protection of capital from undue risk."
The prospectus actually contradicts its own stated objectives and admits that it doesn't always take a "prudent approach." It says:

These risks include higher likelihood of default by the issuer, greater price volatility, difficulty of disposing of or valuing the securities under certain market conditions.

Protection of capital from undue risk?

Don't even bother reading the "Objectives" section. The principal objective of many funds is just to get your money.
The prospectus is not a sacred document. It should be read very selectively.

Craig Stock, a financial columnist for the *Philadelphia Inquirer*, selected some statements from actual prospectuses and translated them into English. A few examples.

The fund:

> Amounts payable under the 12b-1 plan need not be directly related to expenses actually incurred by the sponsor on behalf of the fund.

Stock's translation:

> We can spend the money we take from you any way we like. We don't actually have to use it for the purpose we've stated.

The fund:

> Although the investments selected for the fund are generally attractively priced relative to cash flow, the companies may occasionally have only moderate reported earnings. This investment approach requires a long-term outlook and may require shareholders of the fund to assume more risk and have more patience than investing in the securities of larger, more established companies. There is no assurance that the Fund will achieve its investment objective.

Stock's translation:

> Some of the companies we invest in are not making much money, and you may not either for a long time. But trust us.

The fund:

> The aggressive investor was rewarded in 1993. (Our fund's) defensive investment discipline is not aggressive.

Stock's translation:

Compared with competing funds, ours stank up the joint in 1993.

Now for the good news.

Your attention has been invited to two parts of the prospectus: financial highlights and fees and expenses.

That is all you have to bother with. You now have the significant facts. One day, when you have become very sophisticated and more familiar with financial terminology, you can—if you feel particularly masochistic—read the rest of the prospectus. Most of it is not very important, and some of it is obscured by legal doubletalk that is simply not worth trying to understand.

Just one more example:

Here is a paragraph from the prospectus of the Dreyfus Growth and Income Fund:

> The effectiveness of purchasing or writing stock index options will depend upon the extent to which price movements in the Fund's portfolio correlate with price movements of the stock index selected. Because the value of an index option depends upon the movements in the level of the index rather than the price of a particular stock, whether the Fund will realize a gain or a loss from the purchase or writing of options on a index depends upon the movement in the level of stock prices in the stock market generally, or, in the case of certain indexes, in an industry or market segment, rather than the movement in the price of a particular stock.

Really?

(You will be overjoyed to learn that there is another paragraph in this prospectus which states that the fund "may or may not" engage in these practices.)

Even John Bogle, chairman of Vanguard, is upset. He said, "Fund prospectuses are largely tedious documents."

Much of the remainder of the prospectus—the part that is still in English—is devoted to various business procedures: how to buy shares, how to redeem shares, how to exchange shares, and so on. Don't waste your time; if you have any questions, call the fund. A human being will eventually respond, and you will find all you need to know without being bored to death.

Say goodbye to the prospectus. Say hello to the statement of additional information.

You have to request this document—the fund will not send it to you automatically when you ask for a prospectus.

You should get it and look through it, even though it is more unclear than the prospectus.

A shareholder recently sued a fund because it had levied a charge against him which was not covered in its prospectus. The court held that because the prospectus stated that there were more expense details available in the statement of additional information, the investor had no basis for his complaint, and the case was dismissed.

The investor had read the prospectus. He had not been told that he also must read the statement of additional information which was not supplied to him. Some legal scholars read the court's opinion and burned their law books.

Legally, the statement of additional information is a supplement document to the prospectus. Most of them are unreadable. The statement of additional information provided by the Transatlantic Capital Growth Fund, for example, contains 43 single-spaced pages.

Still, as I said, you ought to look through it. Sometimes—not often—the attorneys preparing these documents fail in their sworn duty to confuse the public and a few simple, declaratory sentences may appear. Conceivably, there is an occasional nugget that may prove useful to you.

If you are an investor in a given fund, you will automatically receive the quarterly, semi-annual, and annual reports. If you are considering investing in a fund, be sure to write and request these documents. Among other things, you will find a list of the fund's holdings. (Morningstar and Value Line both carry this information, but it is often outdated.)

Stand back.
Let us try to review the essence of this chapter.

1. You need to focus on just two sections of a prospectus: the financial highlights and the fees and expenses.
2. A typical prospectus is a mass of confusion and not worth trying to navigate. As the *Philadelphia Inquirer* wrote:

   Arthur Levitt, chairman of the Securities and Exchange Commission, yesterday told mutual funds in clear, plain English that he wants them to dump the jargon and talk to investors in—clear plain English.

   Mr. Levitt was quoted as having said:
   The prose trips off the tongue like peanut butter. Poetry seems to be reserved for claims about performance.

If the chairman of the Securities and Exchange Commission is upset by not being able to understand all the legalese and doubletalk, why should you bother? You are not going to make your purchase only on the basis of the information supplied by the fund. Pick out the few facts that you really need to do your own research.

The real value of the prospectus is highly overrated.

Ten

Introduction to the Model Portfolios

Overview and Ground Rules

1. Only funds rated 4 or 5 stars by Morningstar will be considered. Why would you invest in anything but the best?

2. Only no-load funds will be considered. An exception may be made for some low-load funds.

3. All the statistical information in these chapters is available in the *Morningstar Mutual Fund Reports*. You should subscribe to Morningstar (call 1-800-876-5005). You can't be home without it. The cost for a year's subscription is $395, and you can purchase a three-month trial subscription for $65. Every two weeks, you will get a booklet containing detailed information about approximately 150 funds. At the end of 20 weeks you will have received information covering some 1,500 funds. The process then starts all over again, updating the information about the funds.

4. The purpose of these chapters is not to give you a series of prepackaged model mutual fund portfolios. The purpose is to explain the process. Predigested model portfolios are of little value because one size does not fit all. The idea is that once you see how it is done, you can do it yourself.

5. A thumbnail sketch of each of the funds under consideration helps eliminate the weaker funds in each category and select the stronger ones for comparison against one another in the final elimination.

Eleven

The Conservative Portfolio

Balanced Funds

These funds seek capital preservation, current income, and long-term capital growth through a mixture of stocks and bonds.

Total number of funds:	43
Funds with 4- or 5-star ratings:	19
Funds with front-end loads:	9
Funds with excessive minimum requirements:	1
Closed funds:	0

The remaining nine funds: 19 funds with 4- or 5-star ratings, minus 10 funds that do not meet the indicated requirements.

CGM Mutual

Portfolio manager Ken Heebner has got religion. For now.

He was slaughtered in 1994 by big bets on high-multiple stocks and bad bets on the direction interest rates would take. He swore off most of his high fliers in early 1995 and moved into a more defensive position. But Morningstar scratched beneath the surface and found—the real Ken Heebner. It said:

Investors shouldn't be fooled by this fund's current conservatism. It never stays in the same place for long and it's apt to get more aggressive as the opportunities arise.

Just what a conservative investor doesn't want.

Columbia Balanced

Although a relatively new fund (founded in 1991), this fund has already taught its peers some valuable lessons. It has found the ideal balance between dividend-oriented issues and higher-multiple growth stocks—all while maintaining a below-average risk rating. Add an expense ratio that is also below average for the category, and you have a clear candidate for the finals.

Dodge & Cox Balanced

Since the mid-1980s, this fund has performed significantly above the average of its group in all but one year. Its return in 1991 pushed it to the bottom of the category, but since then it has finished well up in the top quintile. On the stock side, it looks for temporary undervalued companies with strong growth prospects; on the bond side, its selections have kept the income stream well above that of most other balanced funds.

Morningstar said, "It's a fine option for one-stop investment shopping."

A finalist.

Evergreen Foundation

This fund has the best three-year record of any fund in its group, despite the fact that its bond holdings were clobbered during the interest rate increases in 1994. Great stock picking cushioned those bond losses, and the fund's fixed-income holdings were considerably revised. In 1995 it was positioned to produce the kind of total results that makes it a clear candidate for the finals.

Fidelity Balanced

This fund can't make up its mind how much it wants to gamble. It has severely reduced its equity positions because of high prices and high market risk. On the other hand, it is buying bonds all over Europe and in South America and adding foreign equity issues as well. Hardly the profile of a truly conservative fund.

Fidelity Puritan

A long, long history of above-average results has made this fund one of only three 5-star funds in the group. It is also one of the few balanced funds to have shown a profit in 1994. And it ended each of the years from 1992 to 1994 in the top quintile of its category. Its basic strategy is to minimize losses and find profits in an eclectic variety of equity issues. A top contender for top honors. A finalist.

Founder's Balanced

This fund is slightly out of balance. Rather than chase yield, it focuses on capital appreciation, resulting in a dividend payout that is considerably and constantly below that of its peers. That strategy might be acceptable if its capital enhancement record were a great counterbalancing force. But it is only slightly better than average, and total returns do not provide the best of either world.

T. Rowe Price Balanced

You have to be impressed if you look at the results of this fund over time. But its outstanding performance was not achieved by the present T. Rowe Price fund alone—the fund was merged into the older USF&G fund and thus acquired its stellar history. The Price Balanced Fund is only a few years old, and its record is benefiting from the prior achievements of its predecessor. Until it establishes a record of its own, the Price is not right.

Vanguard Wellington

This fund looks great. It is one of the oldest and largest balanced funds and has one of the better records. But trouble lurks ahead. If interest rates spike up again, this fund will spike way down because of its unusually large stake in rate-sensitive bonds. And should the equity market run into even temporary trouble, Wellington's overweight in cyclicals could cause an ocean of red ink. The future is too uncertain to be certain about this once great fund.

The Finals

Four funds remain: Columbia Balanced; Dodge & Cox Balanced; Evergreen; and Fidelity Puritan.

Columbia Balanced is the first to be eliminated, solely because it is too new. Although its short life has been a happy one, it has not yet been tested for the difficult times that may lie ahead. A profitable record over an extended period is a requirement when you get down to the final wire.

The portfolio of Fidelity Puritan simply does not measure up to that of its competitors. It is overfocused in two chancy areas: oil and Japanese securities. If either, or both, run into any kind of trouble, Puritan is not sufficiently diversified to staunch the bleeding.

Evergreen has been lucky. Its total return record has been excellent, but a little deceptive. It suffered serious losses with its fixed-income issues, losses that were hidden by unusually good fortune on the equity side. It has a worrisome 27% of its assets in long Treasuries, in an interest rate environment that is far from settled. Great stock selections may have saved it once, but two-peat is too much to expect.

Dodge & Cox, on the other hand, has shown very strong

equity returns and a dividend stream that is well above average. It does not have an undue concentration in any fixed income area. It was one of a very few funds to show a profit in 1994, and it has never had a losing year. All this, with a below-average risk rating. The clear winner.

Equity Income Funds

These funds seeks both current income and capital appreciation.

Total number of funds:	33
Funds with 4- or 5-star ratings:	13
Funds with front-end loads:	8
Funds with excessive minimum requirements:	0
Closed funds:	0

The remaining five funds:

Fidelity Equity-Income I

The principal thing wrong with this fund is its sibling—Fidelity Equity-Income II. While it has a fine history on its own, it suffers by comparison in the important bottom-line measurement of total return. Although its 2% load is not a deterring factor, you get better performance without any load with the newer fund. Investors seem to have recognized the difference: in less than four years, Equity-Income II developed a much larger asset base than its much older family member.

Fidelity Equity-Income II

This is the only 5-star-rated fund in the group, and with good reason. It has been in the top quintile of its category each year since 1991. And portfolio manager Brian Posner has made more good moves than Michael Jordan. He took profits in cyclicals and moved into basic industries. He took his profits there, sold out, and went back to the cyclicals, which were then available at cheaper prices. He also got into the energy sector just before fuel prices skyrocketed. A vote for the man with the Midas touch. A finalist.

Invesco Industrial Income

Trouble. Long-time portfolio manager John Kaweske was fired for allegedly violating the rules of personal investing. His successor now has to match or beat a standout record and has not had enough time to make his presence felt. As of this writing, his selections have been uninspired and the results uneven. This fund may have seen its best days.

T. Rowe Price Equity Income

The best of both worlds? This fund has recently produced strong records in both capital appreciation and yield. It is also a venturesome fund, successfully moving into health care and consumer staples, sectors normally avoided by most equity income portfolio managers. And its fixed income side is well balanced between high-coupon issues and a careful selection of Treasuries. A finalist.

USAA Mutual Income Stock

High marks in yield, mediocre marks in capital appreciation. Its fixed income success has been wasted by mistakes and misfortunes on the equity side, particularly in financials and electric utilities. The payoff in total return does not compare with that of other funds in the group that are much more successful with their balancing acts.

The Finals

The choice is between Fidelity Equity-Income II and T. Rowe Price Equity Income.

These funds have almost the same record, the same investment outlook, and the same management style, and their portfolios offer little choice. In such a tie-making circumstance, the vote has to go to Fidelity, the only 5-star fund in the group. It has the significant advantage of Fidelity's enormous research capacity and the fact that Fidelity always seems to get the news first about pending market changes. You won't go wrong with the T. Rowe Price fund; you just figure to do a little better with Fidelity Equity-Income II.

Government and Corporate Bond Funds

The next step is to select a government bond fund and a corporate bond fund in order to give conservative investors a choice between pure safety and safety with an opportunity for some capital appreciation. Because safety is the primary consideration, only funds rated 5-star will be considered.

Government Bond Funds

Of the 56 government bond funds rated by Morningstar, only four have earned its 5-star rating: Dreyfus Short-Term Intermediate Government; Fidelity Spartan Limited Maturity; Sit U.S. Government Securities; and Strong Government Securities.

How can there be 52 other funds, all investing in government securities, that have not earned the highest Morningstar rating? Aren't they all investing in guaranteed instruments? Can one be less safe than another?

It is not only a question of safety. It is also a question of the maturity dates of the paper, which are more—or less—vulnerable to changing interest rates; the mix between pure Treasury instruments and other government-type paper; and the manner in which earned income is distributed.

The first of these four funds to be eliminated is Strong Government Securities. As Morningstar says:

All five-star government general funds are short-ma-
turity, conservative offerings, with one exception: this
fund.

Yes, there is risk, even in government bond funds. Some,
like this one, deal in such exotic offerings as inverse floaters and
principal-only strips. These are perfectly legitimate investments,
but not as rock-ribbed conservative as the normal holdings of
most funds in this category.

The Dreyfus Short-Term Intermediate Government Fund is
eliminated for much the same reason, although the explanation
is more difficult to follow. This fund deals in a lot of premium
coupon bonds which can reduce net asset value as they approach par.

How's that again? Is the average investor supposed to understand that?

No. And the lesson is: don't select a fund whose practices
and procedures you don't thoroughly understand, no matter
what its previous record may be.

The two remaining funds, Fidelity Spartan and Sit, are very
much alike. However, over time Sit has produced a higher yield
and a higher average return. Says Morningstar:

Trustworthiness, combined with low risk and strong
long-term returns, makes this a choice with which investors can feel comfortable.

A comfortable vote for Sit U.S. Government Securities.

(There are different types of government bond funds. It was
suggested in an earlier chapter that there is no reason to invest
in government Treasury funds because you can buy Treasury
bills, notes, or bonds yourself. The funds referred to here are not
government Treasury funds. Morningstar calls them "government bonds, general," and they do not limit their investments
just to Treasury bills, notes, and bonds.

Corporate Bond Funds

Morningstar has awarded its 5-star rating to nine no-load corporate bond funds.

Three of them are eliminated at once because their portfolios consist of too much low-quality paper. The Invesco Select Income fund has 61% of its money invested in bonds rated less than AAA. Both the Loomis Sayles and the Strong Advantage funds have 83% of assets in these lower-quality bonds.

Remember the watchword: conservative.

That word also eliminates the Fidelity Investment Grade Bond Fund. It took a beating in Mexican and Argentinian issues and strayed far afield (Thailand) in a frantic pursuit of yield. Too many risks to qualify as a truly conservative selection.

The Fidelity Short-Term Bond Fund is even more unconventional than its sibling. It believes in taking on emerging market debt—a precarious strategy for even an aggressive investor. Says Morningstar:

> Those seeking the most conservative of the conservative bond funds should just keep on looking.

The final—and choice—selection is the Harbor Bond Fund. Its holdings give it the potential for moderate appreciation without sacrificing safety. It has run with the bulls without being clawed to death by the bears. It has been in the top quintile of its category in each year since 1991. Morningstar's comment:

> This fund has the best of both worlds. Its returns for the trailing three- and five-year periods rank it in its objective's top quintile and its risk scores sit in the group's safer half.

Summary

Conservative investors come from a very wide variety of financial backgrounds. A 65-year-old widow who has just inherited her husband's modest estate has different financial requirements from a 30-year-old divorced working mother who is trying to build up some future savings. Obviously, all situations cannot be covered, but here are some recommendations:

1. The 65-year-old-widow with a reasonable nest egg:

> 50% Fidelity Equity-Income II
> 25% Dodge & Cox Balanced
> 25% Sit Government Securities

She needs a steady flow of dividends; hence the emphasis on shares in Fidelity Equity-Income II. The Dodge & Cox fund will provide an opportunity for capital appreciation without much downside risk, and the Sit U.S. Government Bond Fund is a safety anchor against any turbulent times.

2. The 30-year-old divorced working mother:

> 60% Dodge & Cox Balanced
> 20% Fidelity Equity-Income II
> 20% Harbor Bond

Her first goal is capital enhancement, which should come from Dodge & Cox Balanced. Her secondary aim of current income will be provided in different ways: Fidelity for dividends from stocks; Harbor for income from bonds.

3. A 50-year-old working couple who can afford to take some modest risk while seeking both capital appreciation and dividend income:

> 33.3% Dodge & Cox Balanced
> 33.3% Fidelity Equity-Income II
> 33.3% Harbor Bond

A third of assets in each of the three funds will provide the diversification necessary to meet the requirements. Capital improvement from Dodge and Cox, income from Fidelity, and some of both from Harbor.

Investors are urged to review their portfolios at regular intervals. As the 50-year-old couple gets closer to retirement age, it should reduce the amount in Dodge & Cox Balanced and seek extra safety with the Sit U.S. Government Bond Fund. The divorced working mother should also make some changes once she has built up a reasonable reserve fund. At that point the safety of the Harbor Bond Fund is no longer necessary, and its allocation should be moved to Dodge & Cox Balanced for additional capital appreciation.

Nothing is forever.

Twelve

The Moderate Portfolio

Growth Funds

These funds seek long-term capital appreciation by investing primarily in common stocks. Dividend income is incidental.

Total number of funds	229
Funds rated 4 or 5 stars:	86
Funds with front-end loads:	33
Funds with excessive minimum requirements:	7
Closed funds:	3

The remaining 43 funds:

Berger 100

This fund is simply too risky for moderate investors. Its volatility is far above average, and its risk scores are among the group's highest, due largely to its concentration in technology and health stocks. Its five-year total returns are satisfying but misleading. It had a sensational 1991 but has been very uneven since, ending 1994 in the bottom quintile of its category.

William Blair Growth

Under new management. The Blair fund was taken over in 1993 by two new managers, and its recently instituted strategy of focusing on small and mid-capitalization stocks has not been tested over the long run. Maybe later.

Columbia Growth

Consistent, but not top-notch. Average risk, average return, average portfolio diversification, average in both up and down markets. A middle-of-the-road fund that offers no special inducement.

Crabbe Hudson Equity

This is a contrarian fund that specializes in finding out-of-fashion companies that the market will eventually (it hopes) recognize. It buys stocks at depressed prices and waits for Wall Street to confirm its choices. Although this strategy has worked reasonably well, it has too much downside exposure to be appropriate for a moderate investor.

Crabbe Hudson Special

The same problem—in spades. A whopping 41% of its assets are in technology stocks—not particularly soothing for the risk-conscious investor. It, too, seeks market rejects and companies in the small-capitalization area. It has even more downside exposure than its sibling.

Delaware Value

A feast-or-famine fund. Bottom of its quintile in 1990; top of its quintile in 1991. Top of its quintile in 1993; bottom of its quintile in 1994. It likes to collect cheap stocks, which sometimes shoot up, but sustained long-term growth normally comes from more substantial holdings.

Fidelity Blue Chip Growth

This fund is misnamed—it is not a blue-chip fund at all. It was once, but when a new portfolio manager took over in 1993, the emphasis was shifted to small and medium-size companies, with a heavy weighting in foreign issues. The name may fool you, but the portfolio is obvious. Not enough quality for further consideration.

Fidelity Contrafund

This fund should change names with its sibling. It is a blue-chip fund, not a contrarian at all. Its portfolio is filled with the stocks of America's biggest companies: IBM, Sears, Intel, Amoco, and Capital Cities, to name just a few. It finished in the top quintile of its category in six out of the last seven years and missed the top ranking in 1994 by a very small margin. Scratch it and it will bleed blue. A finalist.

Fidelity Disciplined Equity

Three computer programs provide the discipline, and the results have been excellent. One model tracks the market's current attitude concerning value; one considers short-term earnings momentum; and the third combines the results of the first two into a plan for action. The results—machine- or manmade—have been above average for years. A finalist.

Fidelity Growth Company

This fund just goes along, year after year, producing top-notch results by investing in top-grade companies. It is difficult not to like a fund that likes General Electric, Pfizer, Johnson & Johnson, McDonald's, Sears, and Chrysler. Its history, portfolio, and management style make it an obvious entrant into the finals.

Fidelity Magellan

The granddaddy of all funds. The single largest of all funds. A true superfund.

A vote for Magellan is like a vote for motherhood and apple pie. How can anyone criticize a fund whose investors have provided an asset base of some $37 billion?

The line forms here.

Ever since the legendary Peter Lynch left, Magellan hasn't been all that great. It made the *Forbes* Honor Roll for three consecutive years while he was running it; since his departure, it has never appeared again. Its new manager, Jeff Vinik, overweighted in technology issues and suffered some painful losses. And Magellan is simply too big—it can't move quickly enough to unload in the uncertain years ahead. Magellan's glory days are over.

Fidelity OTC

The television commercials for Nasdaq have tried to change its reputation as the home of only cheaper stocks. While Fidelity OTC is obviously Nasdaq-oriented, it tends to select only the bigger, more solid stocks on that exchange and supplement them with a sprinkling of blue-chip issues to produce a superior balance. (Motorola, Microsoft, and Intel are not exactly bargain-basement issues.) It's a combination that works. Clearly, a finalist.

Fidelity Retirement Growth

Risk and retirement don't go together. Prior to 1992, this fund took on more risk than its name implies. Its new manager, Harris Leviton, has slowly changed that profile. Its new look is symbolized by its lead holding—IBM—and its willingness to go into cash when the market looks dangerous. With reduced risk, returns improved considerably, and it ended the last two years in the top quintile of its group. A finalist.

Fidelity Stock Selector

When the Fidelity Retirement fund had 27% of its assets in cash, this fund was just about fully invested. Its risk/return ratio is more typical of an aggressive growth fund than a slow, steady growth fund. Too much risk—not enough reward.

Fidelity Value

Less risk and more reward, just the opposite of its sibling. This fund has finished each year since 1992 in the top quintile of its group with below-average risk. Instead of Stock Selector's 17% in technology, Value has only 5%, and the rest of its risk is spread out over a large number of holdings. It has also proved to be very nimble—moving in and out of sectors with the agility of a much smaller fund. A finalist.

First Eagle Fund of America

This eagle hunts bargains. Name the sector—if the price is right, the Eagle will pounce on it. Health care, financials, the defense industry—almost anything that is on sale is prey to its appetite for beaten-up issues. Said Morningstar, "If First Eagle Fund of America made a sound it probably would be 'Cheap, Cheap, Cheap.'"

Founder's Growth

There are few funds in the growth category with a more uneven record. In the bottom quintile in 1988, top in 1989. Bottom in 1990, top in 1991. In the fourth quintile in 1992, bottom in 1993, top in 1994. Do you invest in this fund or buy a see-saw?

Franklin Balance Sheet Investment

This fund has feasted on small cap, low-price/book stocks, and, so far, the diet has proved to be very healthy. Investors don't seem to be worried about the downside risk—its asset base quadrupled in 1994. It was in the top quintile of its category in each of the last three years. Despite its somewhat extreme port-folio, it warrants another look in the finals.

Gabelli Asset

Risk is a dirty word to this fund. It typically spreads its bets over some 300 issues and maintains as much as 40% in cash. And it has outperformed most of its peers since 1992. However, it does have a serious problem. Its founder and portfolio manager, Mario Gabelli, has announced his retirement and no successor has been named to date. We have to wait and see.

Harbor Capital Appreciation

This is a go-go fund masquerading as a growth fund, with 34% of its assets in technology stocks, 12% in the volatile health field, and another 16% in foreign issues. That strategy paid off big in 1991 (plus 57.8%), but since then its performance has been lackluster at best. With an above-average risk rating and the uncertainty facing those high fliers in the years ahead, moderate investors must seek a safer harbor.

Janus

This fund is living on its reputation. It had a number of spectacular gains and almost tripled its asset base in 1992 when it produced a 42.8% profit. Since then—while investors have continued to pour in money—they have not been rewarded by outstanding performance. The fund lost money in 1994, and there is nothing about its portfolio that offers great expectations for the future. In fact, its flight into cash—47% at this writing—is some indication that this fund may have lost its way.

Lindner

Too much small cap exposure and too many European stocks are dangerous components for the sure-footed steadiness required of a growth fund. It has been in the bottom quintile of its group since 1992.

Longleaf Partners

This fund is on a winning streak. It had three great years in a row and was one of the few funds to show a 1994 profit. As Morningstar says, "Its long-term risk/return profile has been exceptional."

An exceptionally easy choice for the finals.

Merger

This is a strange, one-of-a-kind fund. It invests most of its assets in companies that are the object of publicly announced acquisition or other reorganization proposals. It was once known as the Risk Portfolio of the Ayco Fund and still is among the riskiest of all growth funds. Much too wild for a moderate investor.

Neuberger & Berman Focus

Prior to 1995, this fund had three different names. It once was an all-energy stock; now it focuses on just six sectors of the economy: cars, media, health, financials, heavy industry, and technology. That concentration limits choices and causes it to miss some good investments when other sectors rotate into favor.

Neuberger and Berman Partners

Over the years, this fund has had an uneven record. Once in the top quintile, once in the bottom quintile, it mostly has been in the middle for total returns in its category. There is nothing that sets it apart from other average growth funds.

Nicholas

Modest. This fund mostly buys value stocks that don't surge up sharply, even in a rising market. And it stays away from the large-capitalization issues and technology stocks that, in proper balance, can reward investors with significant gains. Nicholas was once a favorite fund of many mutual fund newsletters, but its better-safe-than-sorry posture and disappointing recent returns have caused it to lose its popularity.

Oakmark

This was the hot favorite in 1995. Unlike many funds in its group, it does not believe in bargain hunting. Its holdings include some of the most prestigious names in U.S. industry: Philip Morris, Anheuser Busch, Quaker Oats, Eli Lilly, American Home Products, and Lockheed. This list has been supplemented with a carefully selected collection of value stocks. It has topped the charts since 1992. The finals would be incomplete without Oakmark.

Pimco Advisors Growth

Because it is almost exclusively growth-oriented, this fund had a great 1991 but has been below average since value came back into favor. On balance, it does not have enough balance between the two.

T. Rowe Price Capital Appreciation

Safety first. This fund is very careful. It appears to be afraid to seek capital appreciation if there is the slightest hint of any risk. A quarter of its assets are usually in cash, and it always has large holdings in fixed income securities. No pain, no gain.

T. Rowe Price Growth Stock

Unlike its sibling, this fund will go anywhere and do anything to make a buck—the Far East, Latin America, Europe, small, mid-, and large capitalization stocks. You got it, the Price Growth fund will buy it. Diversification is a great quality, but variety alone is not the spice of life on the stock market.

T. Rowe Price New America Growth

This fund believes that small is beautiful. And it specializes in small companies with high price multiples, a combination that could prove catastrophic in a sustained down market. Unless you can guarantee a bull market forever, you can't afford to buy this fund.

T. Rowe Price Spectrum Growth

This is a fund of funds—it invests only in other T. Rowe Price funds. There are no expenses and the turnover rate is very low, but there isn't much to be gained in buying a fund that buys funds you wouldn't buy in the first place.

Schafer Value

Here is the other side of the coin of many funds I have described. As its name indicates, it is a value fund that underplays—even overlooks—good growth stocks. The result is what you might expect: good years when value is in style; poorer years when growth issues are popular. It ran into a brick wall in 1994 and got defensive. It appears that it will just sit around until value comes back in style.

Schwartz Value

The game's the same—only the name is different. This fund was great during the value years, but before and since, it has had a particularly hard time of it. It invests in the smallest of small companies—obscure, underpriced issues—that may have their day but are very vulnerable to downdrafts. It finished 1994 in the bottom quintile of its group.

Sit Growth

Another entrant in the value-vs.-growth battle—this one with a studied disdain for value stocks. Again, just the results you might expect from a lopsided fund. The ride is too bumpy for moderate investors.

SteinRoe Special

This fund, like so many of its peers with so-so records, likes to shop at Kmart. If a stock is marked down or marked Bargain!, SteinRoe Special will give it special consideration. Its portfolio is a rag-tag blend of underfollowed issues. A bargain is often what you pay for it.

Strong Opportunity

The Strong Opportunity Fund is, indeed, a strong opportunity. It posted three back-to-back finishes in the top quintile of its group and did so with risk ratings among the lowest in the category. It boasts a portfolio that is perfectly balanced between value and growth, making it a sturdy vehicle in all kinds of market weather. A finalist.

Value Line

This fund follows Value Line's famous—and rigid—formula of timeliness. Except that it doesn't always tell the right time. In 1994, for example, the formula said that technology stocks were fading, so it took its losses and got out, thereby missing the sector's big comeback a few months later. It took a particularly big loss in a stock called 3Com, only to watch it hit an all-time high after the sale. In recent years, the value has gone out of Value Line.

Vanguard/Primecap

Here is a true growth fund. It likes to invest in mid- and large cap issues during periods of weakness and then hold on to them for the long term. Since 1993 this strategy has paid off, but there were many earlier famine years when the market looked the other way. The fund is wildly overfocused in technology and service stocks—which it will probably hold too long.

Westcore Midco Growth

This is a small fund that deserves a wider reputation. As its name indicates, it is mostly a mid-cap buyer, closely following the S&P Midcap 400 index. Says Morningstar: "When growth companies and the mid-cap market are in vogue simultaneously, this fund will be one of the best-dressed guests at the ball."

A finalist.

Summary

There are 11 finalists.

All of them are excellent funds, some are great but only one or two are extraordinary. How do we pick the very best?

One way to begin is to eliminate the extremes. Remove the most conservative—Fidelity Retirement Growth—and the most risky—Fidelity OTC.

With some reluctance, Franklin Balance Sheet Investment must also be eliminated, which, frankly, can turn out to be a mistake. Its three-year average return—19.3%—is excellent. It has been in the top quintile of its group since 1992. But its wild overemphasis in low-multiple, small-capitalization stocks is just to scary. As Morningstar says, "The fund lost oodles in 1990's recession-driven correction and could do so again."

Next, remove the funds that have too short a history. That eliminates Oakmark, which is currently being touted as the hot fund for the twenty-first century. Founded in 1992, it still must prove that it is not just a flash in the pan. There are a lot of funds that started off like a house on fire and then cooled off and were forgotten.

The next measurement is a comparison of three-, five-, and 10-year records. This yardstick removes Strong Opportunity,

Longleaf Partners, Fidelity Disciplined Equity, and Westcore Midco Growth. None of them has a 10-year record, and their three- and five-year returns are considerably lower than those of the remaining entrants.

Leaving three: Fidelity Value, Fidelity Growth, and Fidelity Contrafund.

Their three-, five-, and ten-year records are very comparable, but Value's achievements came only after 1992. Over the longer periods, Value's performance is far overshadowed by the other two.

Final judgment: The Fidelity Contrafund has a much more impressive long-term record than Fidelity Growth. It outperformed Growth in each of the three-, five-, and 10-year periods. It is not as overweighted in a few volatile sectors (Growth has 32% of its assets in technology issues), and its risk/reward record is much more comforting than that of its rival. (Morningstar rates the Contrafund as below average in risk. It rates Growth as above average in risk). And the Contrafund was in the top quintile of its category for six consecutive years, a performance history unmatched by any Growth fund.

The clear winner: Fidelity Contrafund.

Growth and Income Funds

These funds tend to be slightly more conservative than pure growth funds; they accent both capital appreciation and dividend flow.

Total number of funds:	126
Funds rated 4 or 5 stars:	48
Funds with front-end loads:	16
Funds with excessive minimum requirements:	4
Closed funds:	1

The remaining 27 funds:

AARP Growth and Income

As befits a fund run by the American Association of Retired Persons, this fund is very conservative. It chases yield more than most, taking on less price risk but severely limiting its growth opportunities. While its dividends provide a cushion against a down market, the bottom line is total return. There are many other funds in this group that deliver excellent dividends and offer a better opportunity for capital improvement.

Babson Value

This is largely a buy-and-hold fund. It owns a limited number of issues and seems to hold on to them through thick and thin—often very thin. In the down year of 1990, when most stocks were sliding, it made little effort to change its portfolio and ended the year in the bottom quintile of its category. This reluctance to get out makes it particularly vulnerable to large losses in bad years.

Burnham

This fund hasn't had a great year since 1987. Much of the time it is trying to make up for mistakes or frantically switching to reduce losses. Its principal talent seems to be picking the wrong sectors at the wrong time. One day, it figures to lose at least one of its four stars.

Columbia Common Stock

Here is a comparative newcomer with a lot of promise. Although founded only in 1991, it has produced better results in its short history than two-thirds of the funds in its category. And it achieved this pinnacle with a below-average risk rating. While it is too early to tell if it has the endurance for the long road ahead, its recent record certainly qualifies it for the finals.

Dodge & Cox Stock

This fund has a simple approach to investing. Its management team pays little attention to the overall economy. The viewpoint is that, no matter what, there are always some good individual stocks that will pay off over time. Its long record has mostly proved the validity of that strategy. And it was one of the very few mutual funds to turn a handsome profit in 1994. A finalist.

Dreman High Return

"High return" is an enticing phrase, but not if shooting the works means shooting yourself in the foot. Dreman is an all-or-nothing kind of fund whose high risk rating will raise your blood pressure. Its up-and-down history is unacceptable if you prefer peace, quiet, and steady returns.

Dreyfus Disciplined Stock

This is really a misclassified index fund. It keeps its sector weightings equal to those in the S&P 500. Its stock selections are more index-driven than those of most other funds—hence the word "disciplined" in its name. Its recent record, however, does not inspire confidence in that rigid investment strategy.

Dreyfus Growth & Income

In just three years, this fund earned four stars—and a reputation for being overly aggressive. It ran up an impressive record in its first two years, then ran into a brick wall in 1994 when it sunk to the bottom of its quintile. Since then, it has become more defensive, which may stem some losses, but it has also changed the venturesome style that made it an early winner. More seasoning is required.

Fidelity

This is Fidelity's oldest fund, and it has not shown many signs of wear and tear. But it hasn't shown any signs of great performance, either. Over the long haul, it has a pretty good record, but that is about all you can say for it. It is an average fund in a category that has some spectacular performers.

Fidelity Growth & Income

Although it carries a 3.0% front-end load, the record of this fund is so outstanding that it warrants further consideration. It was in the top quintile of its category in eight years out of a nine-year period. As Morningstar says, "Fidelity Growth and Income Portfolio is leaving its rivals in the dust—again."

The low load cannot be considered that much of a drawback. A finalist.

Founder's Blue Chip

Pretty good in growth, pretty bad in income. While this fund's record is better than most, its yield is half the group's average. It has relatively little exposure in high-dividend sectors and fewer large-cap stocks, despite its prestigious-sounding name. Its 4-star rating was earned when it was a more conventional fund. Its new style has not yet had sufficient exposure.

Gateway Index Plus

This fund does not deserve its 4-star rating. It got lucky in 1994, but it was in the bottom quintile of its category in each of the preceding three years. Since 1983 it has matched its peers only three times, and it has been in the bottom quintile 50% of the time. Unlike most growth and income funds, it does a lot of option writing. This technique has its charms, but if the underlying index appreciates above the strike price, the fund has to pay out the difference. That could turn a moderate investor into a basket case.

Homestead Value

Another buy-and-hold fund. It buys relatively cheap cyclical stocks and sits tight, waiting for Wall Street to recognize their inherent values. In a reasonably stable stock market that strategy might pay off, but if there are any turbulent times ahead, Homestead Value is not sufficiently flexible to avoid serious downdrafts.

Invesco Value Equity

Up and down. Up and down. Up and down. The results of this fund over the years have been up, down, middle, down, middle, up. It is a computer-driven fund, dear to the heart of technicians but out of touch with the real world.

Lexington Corporate Leaders

This is as blue-chip as you can get. The fund's first 10 holdings are: Mobil, Procter & Gamble, Exxon, Du Pont, General Electric, AT&T, Kodak, Sears, Union Pacific, and Chevron. It hardly ever changes its portfolio and had added only one stock since 1935. If all those stocks collapse, your money won't be worth much anyhow. If you believe in the future of the country, you have to believe in Lexington Corporate Partners. A finalist.

Maxus Equity

What a record! Since 1990 this fund has produced twice the return of the average growth and income fund while keeping a low risk rating. It keeps 13% of its portfolio in convertible bonds and convertible preferreds, which throw off handsome dividends and still hold out the promise of capital appreciation. The fund was in the top quintile in 1993 and held its own in 1994's choppy market. A finalist.

Mutual Beacon

This fund does not belong in the growth and income category. It seeks growth only and pays no attention to stocks paying healthy dividends. Since 1989 it has been in the top quintile of its group half the time and in the bottom quintile the rest of the time. If it walks and talks and quacks like an aggressive growth fund, it is an aggressive growth fund.

Mutual Qualified

A clone of Mutual Beacon. It also had three great years and three very lean years. It also is primarily interested in growth, not in dividends. If anything, it is more vulnerable to down markets than its sibling because it tends to favor lesser-quality stocks. When cheap stocks get cheaper, this fund will go down faster and stay down longer.

Mutual Shares

There isn't a lot of difference among the three funds in this mini-family, and this one doesn't offer much protection against stormy weather, either. While it managed to stay dry in 1994, its previous history is not exactly filled with sunshine. While no investor can be fully protected against market changes, it is comforting to have the anchor of dividends.

Neuberger & Berman Guardian

Lately, this fund has turned itself into a winner, but it has some serious drawbacks. It places enormous bets in what it perceives to be hot sectors and can suffer tremendous losses if that over-weighting turns cold. Its yield is well below average for its category. Its recent record is commendable, but its uncommon style is just too risky for a moderate investor.

Rightime

Rightime is a market timer that buys only other funds. Unfortunately, it doesn't always know the right time. As Morningstar says, "Few market timing funds excel over time and this offering is no exception."

Safeco Equity

Safeco Equity has a great record. It also has a great problem.

Its outstanding performance since 1985 was the result of the unique management style of portfolio manager Douglas Johnson, who left to join Smith Barney. While there are the usual public relations clichés about "maintaining the same fundamental approach," the fact is that you now are in the hands of the second team. There is no history of anyone ever having really replaced Ted Williams.

Scudder Growth & Income

Yield and capital appreciation—this fund manages to produce both without overemphasizing either. It buys preferred stocks and convertible bonds to provide dividends and blue-chip-type issues to deliver capital enhancement. That simple combination has resulted in consistently high performances over the years. Its risk rating and expense ratio are both below average; its dividend distribution and total return are both above average. Welcome to the finals.

SteinRoe Prime Equities

Not bad, but not good enough. You have seen its investment strategy before: forget yield and look for growth only. In seeking this goal, however, the fund ventures into many risky areas where most growth and income funds would fear to tread. And its total return averages are not all that distinguished.

Vanguard Index 500

As the name indicates, this is a true index fund. It mimics the S&P 500 and goes wherever the stock market takes it. It is not, by charter, overweighted in any one sector, which causes it to miss some booms but helps protect it against most busts. Not much excitement—just consistent profitability. Another finalist.

Vanguard Quantitative

This, also, is an index fund—sort of. Instead of mimicking the S&P 500, it tries to beat it by ranking the stocks on that index and selecting only the issues that show earnings momentum, special value, and a discounted cash flow. Unlike a true index fund, it is overweighted in the more explosive sectors, giving it much more volatile action than the typical growth and income fund. And its record against the S&P 500 is not all that exciting.

Warburg Pincus Growth & Income

This is a fund for all seasons. By charter, it is required to invest 60% of its assets in dividend-producing stocks which also, it turns out, have had great growth records. It also seems to have a unique ability to get into hot sectors and get out before they cool off. Investors have voted for this fund with their money—in 1993 its total asset base was only $34.5 million; in 1994, it reached $628 million. This time, we'll go along with the crowd. A finalist.

Summary

There are eight finalists.

The first to be eliminated is the newest—Columbia Common Stock, which has only a three-year record. Sometime in the future—maybe tomorrow, maybe some years from now—the stock market is due for a severe correction. There is no way to know how a fund can handle something it has never experienced.

The next step is to compare the records of the remaining funds over three-, five-, and ten-year periods. That yardstick eliminates Lexington Partner, Maxus Equity, and Vanguard 500. Their long-term records are considerably weaker than those of any of the remaining funds.

The next to go is Warburg Pincus. Its yield is significantly lower and its expense ratio considerably higher—almost double that of the other funds still under consideration.

Leaving Fidelity Growth & Income, Scudder Growth, and Dodge & Cox.

In truth, there is little to choose among them. None is overweighted in any particularly volatile sector; all turned profits in 1994's very difficult market.

The final vote goes to Dodge & Cox because its recent history, management style, and current portfolio are the closest to those of an ideal growth and income fund. It is better balanced between yield and growth, and it is slightly more venturesome. And its long-term total return record is markedley better. As Morningstar says:

> It has shone in both good markets and bad while paying a healthy dividend. All in all, it is an appealing package.

Asset Allocation Funds

These funds seek both capital appreciation and income through a mixture of stocks, bonds, and other money market instruments.

Total number of funds:	36
Funds rated 4 or 5 stars:	17

Funds with front-end loads: 7
Funds with excessive minimum requirements: 2
Closed funds: 1

The remaining seven funds:

Crabbe Hudson Asset Allocation

Very conservative bond selection, somewhat volatile stock selection—that combination has worked well for this fund. On the stock side, it likes slightly scarred issues at bargain prices; on the bond side—up to 50% of its assets—it stays with the tried and true. It is not afraid of cash and has benefited from its ability to read the intentions of the Federal Reserve Board. A finalist.

Fidelity Asset Manager

This is the giant of the asset allocations funds, with assets over $11 billion. But it seems to throw this money around with reckless abandon. It is heavy in emerging market debt, in commodities, in junk bonds, and in small-capitalization stocks. Hardly the profile of a moderate fund that is supposed to offer slow growth with little downside risk.

Flex-funds Muirfield

Market timing is the secret of its success—so far. It uses a series of complex technical indicators to tell it whether the market is safe or risky. That worked in 1994, when it stayed mostly in Treasuries and money market funds. It failed in 1993, and Muirfield fell to the bottom quintile of its category. Market timing may be a great idea, but you have to be right most of the time.

General Securities

Experience. Jack Robinson, who runs the portfolio, has the longest tenure of any mutual fund manager. His battle-scarred experience has mostly paid off. The fund's average returns over the years have put it in the top decile of all the funds tracked by Morningstar. Its portfolio is filled with blue-chip-type stocks. General Securities does not have a lot of downside risk, and it is poised for substantial gains if the market doesn't get too skittish. A finalist.

Seafirst Retirement Asset Allocation

"Safety First" is the motto of Seafirst. It rarely deviates from its mix of 55% stocks and 45% bonds, it does not buy any foreign securities, and it is very conservative in its stock and bond selections. This cautious approach has produced only so-so results. Not much downside risk, but not much significant growth potential, either.

USAA Investment Cornerstone

This fund was originally created as an inflation hedge. In its early years, it focused on gold stocks and real estate issues. When the dangers of inflation faded, it changed its strategy and is no longer a hedge against inflation—just when we might need it most.

Vanguard Asset Allocation

The story of this fund can be summed up by one paragraph from the *Morningstar Reports:*

> The fund's above-average returns, moderate risk and low expenses make it a solid offering for conservative investors.

In a group that generally has trouble deciding how to allocate its assets, the steadfastness of this fund makes it a clear choice for the finals.

Summary

There are three finalists: Crabbe Hudson, General Securities, and Vanguard Asset Allocation.

Despite what Morningstar said, Vanguard Asset Allocation is eliminated because it is the fund most exposed to the danger of any increase in interest rates and because its portfolio does not offer much protection in a down market.

Crabbe Hudson gets the vote over General Securities simply because it is surer and steadier. General Securities delivers a lower yield, a higher risk rating, and a very uneven record by comparison. Morningstar's comment on Crabbe Hudson:

> Management may well be on target with its current portfolio—the team has certainly made lots of good calls in the past.

The Moderate Portfolio

The term "moderate" describes most mutual fund investors. And they represent such a wide variety of financial circumstances that an almost infinite number of model portfolios would be required to cover them all.

The two portfolios recommended here are offered for each end of the moderate scale; the first is on the conservative side; the second is for the more venturesome.

Model Portfolio #1

20% Fidelity Contrafund
40% Dodge & Cox
40% Crabbe Hudson Asset Allocation

Model Portfolio #2

60% Fidelity Contrafund
25% Dodge & Cox
15% Crabbe Hudson Asset Allocation

Thirteen

The Aggressive Portfolio

Aggressive Growth Funds

These funds seek capital appreciation. Risk is part of the process.

Total number of funds:	36
Funds rated 4 or 5 stars:	16
Funds with front-end loads:	7
Funds with excessive minimum requirements:	0
Closed funds	2

The remaining seven funds:

Fidelity Capital Appreciation

This fund should operate out of Filene's basement, not Boston's Dorchester Street, Fidelity's headquarters. It buys cheap stocks in both domestic and foreign markets and has shown an uncanny ability to find the right ones at the right time. It has been in the top quintile of its group since 1992. In this case, a bargain is really a bargain. A finalist.

Founder's Special

This is really a technology fund posing under another name. It has always been overweighted in that sector, leading to occasional (very occasional) spectacular results, but suffering dreadful losses when hi-tech became low man on the stock market's totem pole. There is nothing particularly special about Founder's Special.

Invesco Dynamics

This fund has been consistent—consistently average. In its long history, it has never ended a year in the top quintile of its group, nor has it ever been at the bottom. Perhaps the most unusual thing about Invesco Dynamics is that it has had six portfolio managers in 10 years. A revolving door only goes round in circles.

Kaufmann

As I noted earlier, Kaufmann's advertising leaves a great deal to be desired, but its accomplishments do not. Its investment strategy is highly unusual, including the shorting of stocks—a relatively rare practice among mutual funds. Unlike its peers, it also is very active in the initial public offering market, where its predictions of things to come have met with great success. Kaufmann may be wild, but its returns are anything but tame. The bottom line is the payoff. A finalist.

Strong Discovery

This is not a typical aggressive growth fund. It really belongs in the mild-and-moderate category. Instead of concentrating on small-cap, high-octane stocks that can catch fire, Strong Discovery balances its minor aggressiveness with a lot of blue-chip issues like Xerox and IBM. It also balances its sector weightings as if it were unsure where the big bets should be placed. A stick-in-the-mud fund.

Twentieth Century Ultra Investors

Over the years, this fund has tried to be all things to all people. First, it was a growth fund, then a small-company fund, and, just recently, it was reclassified again. Actually, it doesn't belong in any of those groups, as it is more strictly a technology fund. Aggressive growth investors like risk, but they should prefer a fund that spreads the risk over a larger spectrum.

Wastach Aggressive Equity

The preceding description also applies to this fund. It has an outstanding recent record, based upon the performance of some sizzling technology stocks. (Microtouch quadrupled in 1994.) Like any fund that stays in one sector too long, it also has had a number of disastrous years when the high fliers fell out of favor. Wastach is too dependent upon finding a few hot winners, year after year.

Summary

Just two finalists: Fidelity Capital Appreciation and Kaufmann.

This is an easy one to call. Kaufmann outshines Fidelity Capital Appreciation in all the important areas. Its five-year average return is almost double that of Fidelity. In good times, it hits higher highs—plus 79.4% in 1991, compared to Fidelity's 9.9% gain. In rougher times, it loses less—during the last down year, its loss was half that of Fidelity. Aggressive investors are, after all, aggressive investors, and Kaufmann is a gamble that figures to continue to pay off big.

Small Company Funds

These funds invest in undervalued, underpriced, emerging companies, usually with high multiples and high risk. Investors must fasten their seat belts and expect an exciting ride.

Total number of funds: 98
Funds rated 4 or 5 stars: 40
Funds with front-end loads: 12
Funds with excessive minimum requirements: 4
Closed funds: 8

The remaining 15 funds:

Babson Enterprise II

This fund was started when its big brother, the Babson Enterprise Fund, was closed to investors. It has not lived up to the family name. Because the original fund concentrates in the small-cap area, this one tends to invest in larger companies and has not had the startling advances enjoyed by its sibling. Maybe later, when it grows up.

Baron Asset

This little fund ($60 million) is a big performer. It was in the top quintile of its group from 1992 to 1994 and got there without an overload of high-multiple issues. Its three-year record produced earnings more than twice those of the equity fund average while incurring less risk. It owns speculative issues—hence the gains— but it balances them nicely with more substantial purchases— hence the consistency. A finalist.

Columbia Special

While this fund has a reasonably good track record, it has a new manager who has not been around the track enough. He has made a lot of dramatic sector switches, but it is too soon to make any judgments.

Dreyfus New Leaders

De-fense! De-fense! Dreyfus New Leaders maintains a much larger than average cash position than its peers and figures to look better in down markets. But you don't buy a small-company fund just to cushion against losses. As Morningstar says, "Shareholders shouldn't expect the fund to be as brilliant on the upside."

We won't.

FAM Value

Another great lesson in why you should not buy a fund on past performance alone. In 1992 FAM Value was in the top quintile of its group. Its asset base skyrocketed from $42 million to $220 million—and the new investors got on board just in time to watch it plummet to the bottom quintile. This fund requires patience—something a small-company fund investor does not have a lot of.

Fidelity Low-Priced Stock

The limitations of this fund are too difficult to be overcome in the long term. By charter, it must invest only in stocks priced under $25 a share. With an asset base of close to $2.5 billion, you soon run out of attractive low-priced issues. At last count, it owned 728 stocks and was still awash in cash. The cash stash will help if the market tailspins, but aggressive investors are looking for action, not money market returns.

Heartland Value

The record and the management style of this fund warrant further consideration, but by the time you read this, it will probably be closed. Management has decided to shut the doors when its asset base reaches $500 million. At the rate it has been attracting investors, it probably will be closed before this book is published. (If it is still open, take a good look at it.)

Legg Mason Special Investment

This fund is a bottom-fisher. It looks for sectors that have been severely punished and rushes in to buy all the out-of-favor bargains. That works sometimes, as it did in 1993. It doesn't work other times—as it didn't in 1994, when the fund ended up in the bottom quintile of its group. Growth at a discount sounds great. Delivering it consistently is the difficult part.

Loomis Sales Small Cap

In the three years this fund has been rated by Morningstar, it completed one year in the top quintile of its group, one year in the bottom, and one year in the middle. It has two managers. One handles value purchases, the other growth investments, and the results don't always mesh.

Meridian

Richard Aster Jr., this fund's portfolio manager, likes cash. That careful posture is more becoming to a conservative fund than to a small-company fund, where risk is part of the price of admission. Meridian is well positioned against a market collapse, but if you really believe it is the Year of the Bear, then you shouldn't be in small-company funds in the first place.

Nicholas II

Another example of a fund that does not deserve Morningstar's 4-star rating. Its results since 1988 have been consistently below average, and it seems more concerned with not losing than it is with winning. Limiting risk is not the name of this particular game.

Parkstone Small Capitalization

An aggressive investor isn't turned off by some risk, but this is too much. Its price multiples are sky-high, resulting in dramatic and often disastrous swings. Excitement is the by-product of small-company investing, but panic is not.

PBHG Growth

In the volatile world of small-company funds, PBHG Growth has managed to turn in a very consistent record. It was in the top quintile of its group in 1992 and 1993 and, unlike even most conservative funds, it turned a profit in 1994. In each of the three preceding years, it was at or very close to the top. It is very difficult to find a steadier fund in this topsy-turvy category. A finalist.

Sit Growth

Oh, for the good old days. Sit Growth was a spectacular performer from 1989 through 1991; it then lost its touch, hitting the bottom quintile for the next two years. Risk goes with the territory, but the rewards have not been consistent enough to warrant the constant exposure.

Twentieth Century Giftrust Investors

This is a great fund, but it can be purchased only to make a gift in trust for the benefit of a child or charity.

Warburg Pincus Emerging Growth

"Emerging Growth," in this case, means investing in very small, little-known companies that may or may not grow up to be real winners. The general idea is that if you buy enough cheap stocks, some of them will pay off and cover the losses of most of the dogs. That premise may work—one of these years.

Summary

Only two finalists—many of the great funds in this category are closed to new investors or have initial minimum investment requirements far above most people's means.

The choice is between PBHG Growth and Baron Asset. And it is a landslide victory for PBHG Growth.

Its five-year average return is more than double that of Baron Asset. Its three-year average return is more than half again as large. It has been in the first or second quintile of its group since 1989. It attracted so many new investors that in mid-1994, fund manager Gary Pilgrim considered the possibility of closing the fund. He later decided not to. Aggressive investors should hope that he keeps to his word.

International Funds

Some international funds invest in just one foreign area; others find opportunities all over the globe. All of them carry above-average risk.

Total number of funds:	184
Funds rated 4 or 5 stars:	33
Funds with front-end loads:	18
Funds with excessive minimum requirements:	4
Closed funds:	2

The remaining nine funds:

Foreign Stock Funds

Fidelity Overseas

This fund is an international contrarian. When other foreign stock funds abandoned Japan, it increased its investments there and reaped rich rewards. When other funds were gorging on emerging market issues, it decided that the worst was yet to come and got out before rising interest rates took their toll. It has an instinct for being in the right country at the right time. A finalist.

T. Rowe Price International Stock

Steady as she goes. While this fund hasn't been in the top quintile of its group for 10 years, it has made the second quintile for nine consecutive years, not a small feat for a fund in the perilous world of international investing. Part of the reason is that it has favored European stocks and generally shunned emerging markets and Latin America. Its very low turnover rate indicates its belief in the long term. A finalist.

Scudder International

This fund has had a strange record since 1983. In all that time, it has never finished in the top quintile of its group. It is somewhat less risky than most, and not venturesome enough for the typical international investor who is looking for just a little more daring.

Sit International Growth

If you like the Pacific Rim, you'll love this fund. On a percentage basis, it has more than twice the amount of assets invested in that area of any of its peers. Its portfolio, therefore, is somewhat difficult for the average American investor to follow. Unless you are an expert on Malaysia, you are well advised to look to more familiar areas for international growth opportunities.

Vanguard International Growth

This fund has more than half of its assets in Europe—and the profits to show for some wise investments there. However, its portfolio manager has announced his intention to cut back that stake drastically and to move much of it to the Pacific Rim. Obviously, he thinks he knows what he is doing. Obviously, we'll wait and see if he does.

World Stock Funds

Fidelity Worldwide

This fund's lead investments are in the United States, the Netherlands, and Japan. It had some extensive holdings in Mexico but cut them back considerably before the bottom fell out of the peso. It seems to have a magic touch when it comes to getting out of hot areas—sometimes a little early—before real trouble sets in. As Morningstar says about portfolio manager Penelope Dobkin:

> Dobkin may not let investors ride to the edge of a rally, but neither does she let them drop off. This offering has so far proved to be a superior world stock investment.

A finalist.

Founder's Worldwide Growth

There aren't many worldwide funds with a consistent record of superior performances. One reason is that there aren't many worldwide funds that have been in business for a long period of time; only a third of the funds in the category have five-year records. Founder's Worldwide Growth has been at it longer than most and has a reasonably even record over many years. And its risk scores are among the lowest in the category. A finalist.

Janus Worldwide

The investment techniques of this fund are different from those of most international funds. It is primarily concerned with a country's overall economic prospects. After a given country is judged to be prosperous or rebounding, the fund looks for prospective investments. If a country is in a recession or heading downward, the fund will not touch any of its stocks, no matter what the prospects may be for an individual company. It seems to work—Janus Worldwide ended 1994 ahead of 94% of its peers. A finalist.

Pacific Funds

T. Rowe Price New Asia

Two losing years in a row are not exactly a great recommendation. This fund invests in cheaper stocks along the Pacific Rim, and it has paid the price for its insistence upon bargain hunting. Portfolio manager Martin Wade may not be right, but he sure is stubborn. He has decided to stay with most of his losing selections because he believes that someday, eventually, the market is bound to turn his way. Maybe. And maybe not.

Europe Funds

There are only three funds in this group that are rated four stars or above. Two of them have front-end loads, and the third has an excessive minimum investment requirement.

Summary

There are five finalists: Fidelity Overseas, Fidelity Worldwide, Founder's Worldwide Growth, Janus Worldwide, and T. Rowe Price International.

The first to go is Janus Worldwide, even though it is one of the few 5-star funds in the group. It simply isn't seasoned enough. Just four years old as of this writing, it does not have the long and distinguished record of the other finalists, nor has it produced the kind of spectacular results sported by many of its rivals.

The T. Rowe Price International Fund has a long record, but it is spoiled by too many losing years. It had back-to-back losses in 1993 and 1994 and a losing record in three out of the last six years.

The three- and five-year total return record of Fidelity Overseas doesn't begin to compare with its remaining rivals. And, it, too, has had three losing years out of the last six.

Leaving Founder's Growth and Fidelity Worldwide.

The decision, by a knockout, goes to Fidelity Worldwide. It has been in the top quintile of its group for three of the last four years while Founder's Growth had back-to-back losing years in 1993 and 1994. Founder's Growth also tends to invest in smaller-capitalization stocks, making it more vulnerable to downside movements, a constant problem in the chaotic world of international investing. Furthermore, Founder's Growth is over-weighted in Europe, while Fidelity Worldwide has spread its risk more evenly over many productive areas.

Model Portfolio

33.3% PBHG Growth
33.3% Kaufmann
33.3% Fidelity Worldwide

By definition, an aggressive investor is willing to take on considerable risk. The wisest course of action, then, is to spread the risk equally. Each of these funds has a superior record, experienced management, and a portfolio balance that should outperform all other funds in its category. Together, they provide a diversification that figures to reap the most benefits from a climbing stock market and soften the downside against the corrections that will inevitably occur.

More than any other portfolio, this one will require a lot of attention. There will be volatility. There will be trying times. But the sun will shine again, and, unless the sky falls in, the potential profits will be worth the gamble.

Afterword

My telephone number is (215) 572-0665.

I will be glad to talk to you.

(Please call at a decent hour. Any time between 9:00 A.M. and 9:00 P.M. Eastern Standard Time.)

If you would like some advice on mutual funds, I will be happy to provide it. No charge.

If you have any questions about any part of the book, I am available to try to answer them.

If you are a stockbroker or a banker or a mutual fund newsletter publisher and you just want to yell at me, that's okay, too. If you manage a mutual fund portfolio and you think I have been unfair or unreasonable or just ugly, I am prepared to defend my position. And I will try to make amends for any factual errors, if any have occurred.

Of course, if you enjoyed the book, then I certainly would like to hear from you. I wrote a book on the stock market in 1985, and I still get occasional letters from satisfied readers. They are manna for my soul. The second greatest joy in the world is writing a good sentence. The third is finding someone to appreciate it.

I am also on Prodigy. You can reach me at mapr36a.

Index